This Book is Donated in Memory of:

KATHERINE
ELIZABETH
PERKERSON

LIFE IN A MEDIEVAL
CASTLE

Tony McAleavy

CONTENTS

THE CASTLE IN WAR AND PEACE

The people who lived in castles were warriors. Even in peacetime they obeyed loyalties and conventions related to warfare. During armed conflict castles occupied centre stage as the focus of sieges; in peacetime they reinforced royal authority as the seat of local government.

THE DECLINE OF THE CASTLE

Many castles fell out of use soon after they were built. Kings and nobles gradually adopted a less itinerant lifestyle and preferred to live in more spacious, conveniently located palaces. The remains of castles continued their inexorable decline until the nineteenth century, when a concerted effort was made to preserve the medieval heritage for the future.

First American Edition published in 2003 by
Enchanted Lion Books
239 Central Park West, New York, NY, 10024
Copyright © 1998 English Heritage
Edited by Kate Jeffrey
Designed by Martin Atcherley
Picture Researcher: Dana Phillips
Historical Consultant: Brian Davison
All Rights Reserved
Printed in the European Union by Snoeck-Ducaju & Zoon
A CIP record is available from the Library of Congress
ISBN 1-59270-005-5

FRONT COVER ILLUSTRATIONS *Left: woman bathing, an example of the privileged in medieval society. Centre: a castle under siege. Right: a king and queen entertain at the high table. Bottom: jousting, a favourite activity of young noblemen*

TITLE PAGE *The siege of a medieval castle*

THIS PAGE *A reconstruction drawing of Kenilworth Castle, Warwickshire in the early thirteenth century*

LIFE IN A MEDIEVAL CASTLE

MEDIEVAL CASTLES CAN STILL BE SEEN throughout the British Isles. In their heyday they were homes to the wealthiest and most powerful members of society: royalty and the great nobility. Within castle walls, these privileged people enjoyed a level of luxury beyond the reach of most medieval men and women. They displayed their wealth through the holding of sumptuous banquets and the maintenance of large households of retainers and servants. They were a restless people, constantly travelling from castle to castle. As they moved about the country, monarchs and nobles exercised governance and dispensed justice. Great lords were, for the most part, little interested in intellectual pursuits and they devoted as much of their leisure time as possible to hunting and preparing for war.

The first part of this book describes the household of a great castle. The personnel of a castle was complex, with many different, specialist posts. Towards the top of the castle hierarchy was a small number of leading officials: stewards with oversight of catering and estate management, a marshal to supervise transport and a chancellor or chaplain to provide administrative support. In addition, there were great numbers of humbler servants such as cooks, carters, grooms and huntsmen. This was a very masculine world: apart from the ladies of the great family and their maids there were hardly any women in the castle household.

The second and third parts of the book consider the evolution of castles and their role in society. Although there were castles before 1066, the arrival of William the Conqueror led to a great proliferation of castle-building. Most of these Norman castles were built not by the king, but by his leading barons, as part of the feudal system. Barons owed loyalty and military service to their feudal overlord, the king. In return they received land, which they controlled from their castles. For strong kings, such as William the Conqueror and Henry II, the system worked well. When royal power was weaker, as in the reigns of King Stephen and King John, the great nobility could use their castles to challenge the power of the king. Castles housed both the highest and the lowest members of feudal society; royal castles were often county gaols, and could be home simultaneously to members of the royal family and local criminals being kept on remand before they were tried.

The final section of the book traces the slow decline of the castle. Changes in warfare and society meant that castles in much of England were largely irrelevant by the end of the Middle Ages. Increasingly, kings and great nobles preferred the greater comfort of grand houses and palaces. A long period of decay began, briefly interrupted by the Civil War in the seventeenth century. Later, castle ruins came to be appreciated for their romantic qualities, and measures were taken to preserve them for future generations, a tradition that continues today. Using the great wealth of surviving documentary and archaeological evidence this book brings the ruins to life, by describing the world of the medieval castle.

MAIN PICTURE *An imaginary scene of bustling activity within the walls of Totnes Castle, Devon. The castle bailey is full of buildings, while the keep (in the background) towers above*

ON THE MOVE

ABOVE *Henry II as shown on his royal seal. Powerful monarchs were constantly on the move*

On 19 March 1265 Simon de Montfort, the Earl of Leicester, arrived at Odiham Castle in Hampshire. His wife Eleanor was already in residence with her staff of about sixty servants. Simon was accompanied by over 100 armed knights, and many more servants. In this way a small castle, which was often almost empty, was transformed into a hive of activity. Grooms had to stable hundreds of horses; the kitchens had to provide catering on a massive scale. Two weeks later the earl and his knights left. They were followed on 1 June by Eleanor and her servants, who went on to Dover Castle. The castle at Odiham returned to its usual sleepy state.

Great nobles such as Simon and Eleanor were a restless, cosmopolitan people. They owned vast, scattered estates and were constantly on the move. As a result of this peripatetic lifestyle a castle which was quiet for much of the year would periodically come alive with the arrival of a large travelling household.

Eleanor was the grand-daughter of Henry II. During Henry's thirty-four years on the throne, he spent Christmas in no fewer than twenty-four different locations on both sides of the English Channel. These Christmas residences included a large number of castles: Lincoln, Marlborough, Oxford, Windsor, Winchester, Nottingham and Guildford. One historian has calculated that great households, such as those of Henry II and the de Montforts, moved on average about once a month throughout the year.

Organising the travelling household of a king or a baron was a challenging

BELOW *A noble household on the move. Left: servants make their preparations for departure. Centre: the lord and lady are accompanied by their entourage. Right: outriders arrive at the destination castle*

ABOVE *A fourteenth-century iron key discovered near the Gate Tower at Leeds Castle, Kent*

task. Peter of Blois, a member of the entourage of Henry II, described the tribulations associated with an itinerant household – especially one whose lord frequently changed his mind about the next move:

> If the king has said that he will remain in a place for a day he is sure to upset the arrangements by departing early in the morning. And you then see men dashing around as if they were mad, beating pack-horses, running carts into one another – in short, giving a lively imitation of hell. If, on the other hand, the king orders an early start, he is sure to change his mind, and he will sleep until midday. Then you will see the pack-horses loaded and waiting, the carts prepared, the courtiers dozing, the traders fretting, and everyone grumbling.

The arrival of the household at a castle must have been an extraordinary sight. A small group of outriders would usually arrive first, ensuring that all was in readiness. In the early twelfth century the outriders of the royal household included two bakers, who could immediately begin cooking bread for the new arrivals. Simon and Eleanor arrived separately, but more typically the lord and his lady with their immediate attendants would follow the outriders together. Travelling separately, and at a slower pace, were carts, pack-horses, hunting dogs and a large crowd of servants.

Travel for a household on the move was slow. When Eleanor de Montfort

moved from Odiham to Dover Castle in June 1265 her entourage travelled about thirty miles a day and spent three nights on the road, staying at Romsey, Chichester and Battle. If a household was engaged in a long journey to a distant castle or palace, an official known as the marshal would try to ensure that the journey could be broken each night in a place of reasonable comfort, such as a large monastery. At Battle, for example, Eleanor presumably stayed at the grand monastery that dominated the Sussex town. On occasion, however, this level of accommodation was not available. Sometimes there was room for the most senior members of the travelling household but not for the majority. Peter of Blois described how Henry II often irritated his household by changing his mind about the intended destination:

> When our courtiers had gone on ahead almost the whole day's ride, the king would turn aside to some other place where he had, it might be, just a single dwelling for himself and no one else. I hardly dare say it, but I believe that in truth he took a delight in seeing what a fix he put us in. After wandering three or four miles in an unknown wood, and often in the dark, we thought ourselves lucky if we stumbled upon some filthy hovel. There was often a sharp and bitter argument about a mere hut, and swords were drawn for possession of lodgings which pigs would have shunned.

ABOVE *An early fourteenth-century enamelled casket made of copper alloy. Caskets were used for the storage of household valuables*

ABOVE *Dover Castle, Eleanor de Montfort's next destination after Odiham in 1265*

WHO'S WHO IN A MEDIEVAL CASTLE

The lord and lady of the household were, when in residence, the dominant figures in the running of a castle. They were attended to by senior members of the household, who were also members of the nobility or gentry.

On the frequent occasions when its royal or noble household was absent, most medieval castles possessed only a very small skeletal staff. Unless there was an unusual level of military activity in the area, garrisons were often quite small. When Odiham Castle was besieged by a French force in 1216, for example, it was held for a week by a garrison of three knights and ten serjeants. The cost of maintaining a

ABOVE *This fourteenth-century drawing shows a meeting of the principal officers of Edward IV's household, including the controller, treasurer, steward and cofferer*

garrison was high and, away from the border areas, sizeable garrisons were rare in peacetime.

The resident staff were headed by the **constable** or **castellan**, who was responsible for the security of the castle. He would be in charge of any military staff present, together with permanent staff such as the **porter**, the **gaoler** and the **watchmen**. The pay of constables varied depending on their responsibilities and the importance of the castle. In 1287 the constable of the Tower of London, the most lucrative position of all, was paid £50 a year, a very large amount in medieval terms. By contrast, the least well-paid royal constable was that of Cambridge Castle who was paid a mere £5. In order to save money the king allowed some constables to

control two castles simultaneously: for example, Bolsover and Peak, Pickering and Scarborough, Shrewsbury and Bridgnorth. Constables were powerful people in the local area and were often feared.

The constable was responsible for the military garrison. After the Norman Conquest a castle garrison usually included **knights**, who owed their lord castle service as part of their feudal relationship (see page 36). The requirement to provide military service was known as 'castle guard'. The length of time served varied from castle to castle, but forty days a year was a typical period.

After the arrival of the royal or baronial household a number of key officials played a major part in the life of a castle:

The **steward** or **seneschal** was originally the person responsible for the organisation of the household's meals in the great hall. This, in turn, gave him oversight of both the kitchens and the estates that supplied the household's food. By the thirteenth century many large households had two stewards – one who dealt with the estates, and another who looked after the feeding of the household. The Scottish Stuart family that came to the throne of England in the seventeenth century were, earlier in the Middle Ages, hereditary stewards to the kings of Scotland. A late thirteenth-century book, known as 'Fleta', detailed the responsibilities of the steward of the household:

> It is the steward's duty to account every night in person or through a deputy, for the expenses of the household, and to ascertain the total of the day's expenditures. It is his duty also to take delivery of flesh and fish of every kind, and this he shall have cut up in his presence and counted as they are delivered to the cook. It is also his business to know precisely how many loaves can be made from a quarter of wheat. Further he should know how many loaves and portions are appropriate for the household on ordinary days.

The **marshal** was in charge of the household's travel arrangements and

ABOVE *The effigy of the great knight William Marshal, from the Temple Church, London. His family were hereditary marshals to the English royal family*

BELOW *The royal castle of Scarborough in Yorkshire shared a constable with nearby Pickering*

the 'outdoor staff', such as the grooms, carters and huntsmen. The family of William Marshal, who ruled England as regent from 1217 to 1219, were hereditary marshals to the royal household. The marshal was a key figure in the household because of the importance of horses in aristocratic life.

The **chamberlain** looked after the bedroom or chamber of the head of the household. He also had oversight of the household valuables. He would be in

ABOVE *This unusual depiction of Richmond Castle in Yorkshire shows the arms of the knights who owed 'castle guard' as part of their feudal obligations*

ABOVE *A king, in the safety of his castle, dictating to two scribes, from a fifteenth-century French illustration*

charge of the clothing and bathing of the lord. One medieval textbook on the organisation of a household gives instructions on how the chamberlain should organise the preparations for the lord's going to bed:

> Take off his robe and bring him a mantle to keep him from the cold, then bring him to the fire and take off his shoes and his hose. Comb his head, then spread down his bed, lay the head sheet and the pillows, and when your sovereign is in bed, draw the curtains. Then drive out any dog or cat, and see there be basin and urinal set near your sovereign, then take your leave mannerly that your sovereign may take his rest merrily.

The **chancellor** or **chaplain** was in charge both of the chapel and the secretarial requirements of the household. This dual function was a consequence of the fact that in the early Middle Ages clergymen had a virtual monopoly of reading and writing. As a result, clerics naturally took on the roles of scribes, archivists and legal advisers. The link between clerical status and writing ability is still evident in the modern word 'clerk', meaning a person whose job involves routine office work. Most medieval households of any size would employ a team of **clerks** to look after administrative matters. One of the clerks sometimes functioned as the household **almoner**, whose job was to distribute charity to the local poor.

From the thirteenth century onwards most noblemen were themselves able to read and write; however, clerks in holy orders continued to provide secretarial support for royal and baronial households.

LEFT *The almoner, with his staff of office, distributing charity to a local poor man*

LORDS AND LADIES

Lords and ladies were at the top of the castle hierarchy, but what sort of relationship did they have with each other? There is evidence that some, at least, of the marriages of the great nobility were happy and stable, including that of Eleanor and Simon de Montfort. Eleanor was the sister of King Henry III, and Simon became the most powerful baron in the realm before his death at the Battle of Evesham in 1265. Their chief residences were Kenilworth and Odiham Castles. They appear to have been devoted to each other and together they formed a formidable partnership. When Simon was away on business, as was often the case, Eleanor ran the household and their estates. On other occasions Eleanor accompanied Simon on his extensive journeys on both sides of the English Channel; for example, Simon went on crusade in 1240 and his pregnant wife accompanied him as far as Brindisi in southern Italy.

Much of Eleanor's and Simon's considerable energy went into efforts to secure the financial future of their children. Eleanor had been married before, at the age of about nine, and she was widowed when she was about sixteen. She then took a vow of chastity, which she broke in January 1238 in order to marry Simon. A son, Henry, was born and baptised at Kenilworth before the end of 1238. Simon and Eleanor may have been lovers before their marriage. In 1239 Henry III argued with his brother-in-law and said, 'You seduced my sister before marriage, and when I found out I gave her to you in marriage, though against my will, in order to avoid scandal.'

If the marriage of Simon and Eleanor was a love match it was unusual at this level of society. Most noble and royal marriages were arranged business transactions. Typically, women married older men. Many girls married when they were in their teens and they were often betrothed even younger. Men were more likely to marry after they had come of age or acquired some property. The age difference often led to women being widowed. As widows they were allowed to keep, for the rest of their lives, one third of the estates of their husbands. Most young widows

ABOVE *Carving of Isabella Forz, the young widow who became a powerful and wealthy woman in her own right*

remarried, although some clearly enjoyed their independence and remained single. One powerful widow was Isabella Forz, Countess of Devon and Aumale (1236–93). Isabella was thirteen when she married William Forz. She had five children and was about twenty-five when her husband died. Isabella refused to remarry. She established herself in Carisbrooke Castle on the Isle of Wight, acquired more land as a result of the death of her brother, and became known as the Lady of the Isle. With a fabulous income of £2500 a year, Isabella was one of the wealthiest people in England. This allowed her to spend a large amount on improvements at the castle and to live in some style. On her deathbed Isabella again asserted her independence by selling Carisbrooke to the king and giving the money to the Church, to the horror of her relatives.

Some marriages were not successful. This was carried to an extreme in the case of Henry II and Eleanor of Aquitaine, the former wife of the King of France. Following the couple's estrangement Eleanor took part in her sons' rebellion against their father in 1173. However, she was captured by her husband's forces as she attempted to join her elder sons, disguised as a man. Eleanor was effectively to remain Henry's prisoner until he died sixteen years later, and for most of this time she was kept under 'house arrest' in Winchester Castle. Her confinement was quite comfortable; she had access to her children and she sometimes

ABOVE *A fourteenth-century depiction of a wedding. At the highest levels of society most marriages were arranged business transactions*

BELOW *The independent-minded Isabella Forz controlled her large estates from Carisbrooke Castle*

ABOVE *An idealised depiction of a medieval king dining in state, from an early four-teenth-century manuscript. The ideal of a harmonious relationship between kings and nobles and their spouses did not always coincide with reality*

travelled, under guard, to other royal residences. Henry II meanwhile fell passionately in love with a woman named Rosamund Clifford. During Eleanor's imprisonment he lived openly with Rosamund, until her premature death in 1176. (Eleanor herself, although eleven years older than Henry, outlived her estranged husband by many years and regained her freedom after his death.)

Henry and Eleanor married when they were both of mature years. Marriages arranged for young children were often, perhaps surprisingly, successful. Sometimes, however, the marriage partners were completely unsuited. In 1344 the Earl of Arundel, the lord of Arundel Castle, obtained an annulment of his marriage. The legal

documents indicate some of the difficulties associated with arranged marriages:

Petition of Richard, Earl of Arundel and Isabella, daughter of Hugh de Despenser – who at the respective ages of seven and eight, not by mutual consent, but by fear of their relatives, contracted espousals, and on coming to years of puberty expressly renounced them, but were forced by blows to cohabit, so that a son was born. They have constantly lived apart, and having provided for their son, petition that they may be free to intermarry with others.

ABOVE *A lover and his lady, from a fourteenth-century French manuscript*

THE CHILDREN OF THE HOUSEHOLD

Most great nobles and members of the royal family saw little of their own children. While very young, children were the responsibility of wet-nurses. At an early age they were often sent to another household in order to learn manners. Castles would, therefore, have contained a number of young people of noble birth in attendance upon the lord and lady of the place. In addition to acquiring social skills young men were trained in hunting and warfare. In the early Middle Ages formal education played little part in the upbringing of children, unless they were destined for a life in the Church. Before the thirteenth century a majority of great nobles were illiterate. Childhood for members of the great nobility did not last long, especially for girls, who often married very young. In the fifteenth century Margaret Beaufort was only thirteen when she gave birth, at Pembroke Castle, to the future Henry VII. Young Margaret had already been widowed before her baby was born.

Kings, queens and great nobles were often anxious about the welfare of their children. In an age when early death was common the future well-being of a dynasty depended on the survival of male children. The financial accounts of Edward I document how on one occasion his son Henry, who was not strong, had a gallon of wine added to his bath. The wine was believed to

RIGHT *This silver bowl, from about 1400, is inscribed with an alphabet and may have been used by a noble child*

have a strengthening effect. He was also prescribed sugar and liquorice by a visiting doctor: in the Middle Ages these luxuries were considered to have medicinal qualities and were thought to be particularly good for chest complaints. Despite these measures, Prince Henry died in 1274 at the age of five.

Given the likelihood of an early death, it was sensible to produce as many male children as possible. This in turn produced another problem – what to do with the younger boys if the eldest survived? Younger sons of great noble families were often steered at an early age into a career in the Church, even if they were completely unsuited to a religious life. Richard de Clare, the Earl of Gloucester and lord of many castles, was one of the most wealthy and powerful barons of the thirteenth century. His eldest son Gilbert inherited his estates and went on to found a magnificent new castle at Caerphilly, arguably the finest baronial castle in Britain (see page 27). By contrast, his youngest son Bogo de Clare was clearly intended for the Church from an early age. In 1255, when Bogo was only seven, he became the rector of two English parishes. This was the start of a spectacularly scandalous career as a money-grabbing, absentee cleric. By the time of his death Bogo held an

BELOW *A boy practises the use of a lance. Such military training was an essential part of a noble boy's education*

astonishing thirty rectorships and twelve canonries. These positions in the Church gave him an enormous income of at least £1000 a year. He entirely neglected his pastoral responsibilities and squandered his income on an extravagant and luxurious lifestyle.

Medieval attitudes to childhood were very different to our own. An incident that took place outside Newbury Castle, Berkshire in 1152 illustrates both the callousness and kindness that could be shown towards medieval children. King Stephen was besieging the castle, which was defended by John Marshal. The king took John Marshal's five-year-old son William as a hostage. Some of Stephen's barons suggested that, unless his father surrendered, the little boy should be placed in a siege engine and catapulted over the castle walls. Others simply wanted to hang William. A message threatening the boy's life by hanging was sent to his father. John Marshal brutally replied that Stephen could kill the boy if he wished for he had a fruitful wife, and had 'the hammer and anvil to forge still better sons'. The king reluctantly ordered William to be hanged from a nearby tree. Little William had no idea what was going on and, at that moment, asked the Earl of Arundel if he could play. Stephen was touched by the boy's innocence and ordered a stop to the execution. Instead of killing the child, Stephen picked him up and took him back to his tent. A few hours later the king's attendants found him playing 'knights' with the boy: this was a game similar to 'conkers', played with plantain stalks. Young William grew up to become the famous William Marshal, one of the most distinguished knights of the Middle Ages.

Sometimes powerful nobles had tempestuous relationships with their children. The children of Henry II saw little of him when they were very young. For example his youngest son, John, was born at Oxford Castle and appears to have spent most of the first six years of his life in an abbey, while his father moved restlessly from castle to castle in England and Normandy. This lack of contact in childhood may account for the fact that all four of Henry's sons took part in armed rebellions against their father when they were adults. Towards the end of his life Henry ordered a wall painting illustrating

the ingratitude of his sons to be put up at Winchester Castle. According to Gerald of Wales, the painting was prominently positioned in the king's private chamber and symbolised 'the tragedy of his life':

There was an eagle painted, and four young ones of the eagle perched upon it, one on each wing and a third upon its back tearing at the parent with talons and beaks, and the fourth, no smaller than the others, sitting upon its neck and awaiting the moment to peck out its parent's eyes. When some of the king's close friends asked him the meaning of the picture, he said, 'The four young ones of the eagles are my sons, who will not cease persecuting me unto death. And the youngest, whom I now embrace with such tender affection, will someday afflict me more grievously and perilously than all the others.'

MENIAL MATTERS

In addition to the major officers, a noble or royal household contained many humbler servants. These people were divided linguistically, as well as socially, from the lord and lady and the great officers of the household. Until the fourteenth century most members of the nobility spoke French as their first language, while English was the mother tongue of the poorer classes.

The grandest of households possessed a great diversity of servants. In the twelfth century the King of England could call upon the services of hundreds of workers including, for example, a fruiterer, a porter of the royal bed and a keeper of the tents. We know of these details from a document called 'The establishment of the king's household', which dates from shortly after the death of Henry I. It lists a bewildering variety of household members. If we look, for example, just at those servants whose work related to hunting, we find that the king had in his entourage:

- hornblowers
  the keeper of the greyhounds and his men
  the keeper of the kennels
  knights-huntsmen
  hunt-servants
  the leader of the bloodhound
  the keeper of the running hounds
  the huntsmen of the stag-hunt
  the huntsmen of the wolf-hunt
  the bowmen and keeper of the king's bow
  the servant who takes in the beasts killed in the chase.

Castle servants were privileged members of society. All members of the household, from the highest to the lowest, received pay, clothes and board and lodging. The household rules laid down by Bishop Grosseteste in the thirteenth century suggest that some servants were also given periods of leave. Since married male members of the household were not usually accompanied by their families, this may have been an opportunity to visit wives and children. The bishop advised lords and stewards to make sure that there were not too

many servants on holiday at any one time.

The daily rates of pay for household members varied considerably. In the twelfth century the humblest workers in the royal household were paid one penny a day. This was very substantially less than the remuneration of the great household officers. At the other end of the scale the chancellor received five shillings a day: sixty times more than the most menial of servants.

Catering dominated the daily functioning of the castle and large numbers of servants were employed in work related to the preparation and serving of food. The cook was usually a servant of some importance, and was paid more than other manual workers. Staff attached to the pantry and the buttery were responsible for the serving, respectively, of the food and drink. Maintaining a store of food could be difficult and sometimes the planning clearly went awry. In 1326 the government ordered the keepers of Nottingham Castle to sell 400 sides

of bacon to local people before they became inedible. Beyond the kitchens and the great hall of the castle, additional servants would be employed in the bakehouse and brewery. Outdoor servants were largely concerned with the running of the stables and other aspects of the transport of the household. Servants of the chamber provided personal service to the royal or noble family. They helped with such matters as dressing and the care of clothes. It was only within the chamber that one would expect to find a significant female presence. A great lady would always have a number of maids and

ABOVE This busy scene shows huntsmen and their hounds. Most great nobles had an extensive retinue of hunt-servants

ABOVE The Luttrell Psalter shows a massive kitchen spit. Castle catering was done on a large scale

BELOW A lady and her maid depicted in the fourteenth-century Luttrell Psalter. The immediate attendants of the lady of the household were among the few female servants in castles

RIGHT *This cutaway reconstruction drawing shows the great hall at Portchester Castle in Hampshire in the fourteenth century. Catering was a major task for the domestic staff in a castle household*

ABOVE *Kitchen and waiting staff at work, from the Luttrell Psalter*

women attendants. While Eleanor de Montfort was at Odiham and Dover Castles in 1265 the only female members of her household were her personal attendants, a laundress called Petronilla and 'an ale-wife from Banbury'. Despite the size of her household Eleanor needed, in addition, to buy in outside expertise. For example, she had to send to Reading for a barber-surgeon to come to Odiham to bleed one of her 'damsels'.

All large households employed a number of messengers. This was an important but hazardous occupation. One of William Marshal's messengers, Richard, was murdered in about 1218 while on an errand for his master. He was attacked near London by a gang of highwaymen who stole his purse and clothes. The St Albans chronicler Matthew Paris recorded how in 1250 a royal messenger was abused in an unusual way by a great baron:

> Walter Clifford, not the least of the barons of the Welsh march, was gravely accused of treating a messenger of the king violently and improperly and of forcing him to eat the royal letters together with the wax seal. Walter did not dare to stand trial, but submitting to the mercy of the lord king, barely escaped death or disinheritance. He lost all the money he had, namely one thousand marks.
> (Matthew Paris)

BELOW *A lady returns a letter to a messenger, from a fourteenth-century manuscript*

CREATURE COMFORTS

C astles had a military function but they were also family homes. Many people today imagine that medieval castles must have been cold, damp and inhospitable. How pleasant in fact was daily life in a castle?

In the early Middle Ages great castles cannot always have been comfortable places, especially for the humbler members of the household. Private rooms, or 'chambers', were only available to a fortunate few. Most people bedded down where they could on portable mattresses. In winter much of the castle would have been cold, and often dark. However, for the head of the household and his immediate associates, life was not necessarily unpleasant and conditions improved during the Middle Ages. In a well-run household hygiene was valued. Access to fresh water was always a crucial factor in the location of a castle, and regular washing and bathing took place, the latter in barrel-type tubs. Surviving accounts show servants being paid extra for the work involved in heating and carrying the water. The travelling household of Henry I included a 'ewerer', who was responsible for the provision of water for washing at meal times and for

organising the king's baths. King John had his own bathman, who was paid a halfpenny daily. He received an extra payment of 5 pence every time the king took a bath. This appears to have happened about once a fortnight. Later some royal castles possessed the luxury of a permanent bath. Official records for 1291–92 include expenses for an elaborate bath built for the king at Leeds Castle in Kent. The costs relate to payments for lead, 100 Reigate stones and the labour associated with the paving of the bath.

Most castles lacked the sophisticated water systems found in medieval monasteries and relied on water drawn from wells. A small number of medieval castles had some form of piped water. Henry II introduced an elaborate system at Dover. The new keep was supplied with water through a well that was dug deep into the chalk below the castle. The water was then piped through from the well-head to other parts of the keep.

The floor of the great hall was covered with rushes which needed to be changed regularly. A twelfth-century

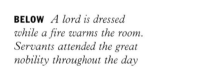

16

writer commented favourably on the cleanliness of the great hall of Thomas Becket, when the future saint was chancellor to Henry II:

LEFT *The decoration from medieval castles has, for the most part, disappeared. These rare wall paintings are from Longthorpe Tower in Cambridgeshire*

> He ordered his hall to be strewn every day with fresh straw or hay in winter and with green rushes or leaves in summer, so that the host of knights who could not find room on the benches might sit on a clean and wholesome floor without soiling their precious clothes and fine underwear.

In the first castles the hall was heated by the fire from a central hearth with a louvered opening in the roof above to allow the smoke to escape. The use of fireplaces became common in halls in the late twelfth century – examples from this period can still be seen in the halls of Rochester and Colchester Castles – although fireplaces in private rooms are not commonly found in castles until the thirteenth century.

Surviving documents from the time of Henry II suggest a high level of attention to comfort and pleasure in many royal castles. They describe expenditure on, for example:

ABOVE *A fifteenth-century stained glass window shows the barrel-type baths used by the wealthier classes*

❖ a painted chamber for the king at Winchester;
❖ gardens at Arundel, Marlborough and Winchester;
❖ dovecotes at Nottingham;
❖ fish-ponds at Newcastle-under-Lyme.

Little is known of the sanitary arrangements in the first timber motte-and-bailey castles. We do know that even the earliest stone castles were usually well provided with latrines or 'garderobes'. Garderobe chutes can be seen on the exterior walls of many castles. These transported waste away from residential areas into ditches, pits or watercourses. Henry II's keep at Dover, for example, was well provided with lavatories. The principal bed-chamber on the second floor had its own 'en-suite' garderobe. The waste from the garderobes of the keep was deposited in a pit which could be emptied from outside the building.

Further developments in the quality of castle life took place in the thirteenth century. During the long reign of the unwarlike Henry III increasing attention at royal castles was given to comfort and interior design. Glazed windows became more common. The use of inlaid floor tiles spread. Henry spent substantial amounts of money on wall paintings for his castles and palaces. In the great hall at Winchester he ordered paintings of the World Map and the Wheel of Fortune. A painting depicting the story of Alexander the Great decorated the queen's chamber at Nottingham

Great households could afford a range of imported luxury goods. In 1286, for example, the royal household used 28,500 pounds of almonds and 6600 pounds of rice. The rice was probably imported from Spain. Other imports came from further afield. The accounts of Eleanor de Montfort in 1265 show her officers on one occasion purchasing 8 pounds of pepper, 6 pounds of cinnamon, 1 pound of cloves, 12 pounds of sugar and 6 pounds of powdered sugar with mace.

Unfortunately for us, very few castle residents committed their thoughts to paper. One exception was Gerald of Wales, a writer and cleric who lived in the late twelfth and early thirteenth centuries. He was brought up in the family castle at Manorbier, on the coast of Pembrokeshire. Later he fondly recalled the scene of his childhood, in a way that suggested that it was a relatively civilised place:

> It has a fine fish-pond under its wall, as conspicuous for its grand appearance, as for the depth of its waters. There is a beautiful orchard, enclosed on one side by a vineyard, and on the other by a wood. Between the castle and the church, near the site of a very large lake and mill, a rivulet of never-failing water falls through a valley.

ABOVE *The floors of the most important rooms were often decorated with ceramic tiles, such as these fourteenth-century examples from Tring in Hertfordshire*

BELOW *Gardens were important as places of recreation, as this late medieval illustration shows*

HOSPITALITY AND ENTERTAINMENT

In the early Middle Ages the central focus for the life of the household was the great hall. Here the household expressed its collective identity and its sense of hierarchy through communal dining. In the thirteenth century Bishop Grosseteste of Lincoln advised the Countess of Lincoln that she should dine with all her household as often as possible:

> Make your own household to sit in the hall as much as you may, and sit you ever in the middle of the high board, that your visage and cheer be showed to all men. So much as you may without peril of sickness and weariness, eat you in the hall afore your many, for that shall be to your profit and worship.

The bishop's advice refers to the fact that the lord and lady of a castle were placed on a platform, or dais, together with their most important guests and officers. This 'high table' was served first. The rest of the company sat at tables in the main body of the hall. Such practices are still reflected today in the dining halls of Oxford and Cambridge colleges. Most people shared dishes with a neighbour – only diners at the high table could expect a dish to themselves. The household almoner was responsible for the collection of left-overs and their distribution to the local poor. Unsurprisingly, great banquets attracted hangers-on and people who were not entitled to hospitality. A royal household order of 1279 instructed the ushers of the hall to 'take care that the hall is well cleared of strangers and ribalds that ought not to eat'.

Great communal meals constituted a considerable challenge for the kitchen staff at a castle. They were responsible for catering on an enormous scale and needed facilities and supplies to match. King John ordered that the new kitchens at Marlborough and Ludgershall Castles in Wiltshire be large enough to roast two or three oxen at the same time. Household accounts detail the huge amounts of food required by castles. These indicate not so much the greed of medieval people, as the size and complexity of the castle household. At the end of the Middle Ages, the Earl of Northumberland's household consumed annually:

- ❖ 16,932 bushels of wheat
- ❖ 27,594 gallons of ale
- ❖ 1646 gallons of wine
- ❖ 124 beef cattle
- ❖ 667 sheep
- ❖ 14,000 herring.

Formal banquets were used by kings and barons to demonstrate their power and wealth to the world at large. William of Malmesbury's summary of the career of William the Conqueror emphasised the importance of the banquets held at the time of the great religious feasts: 'He gave sumptuous and splendid entertainments at the principal festivals. At these times a royal edict summoned thither all the principal persons of every order, that the ambassadors from foreign nations might admire the splendour of the assemblage, and the costliness of the banquets.' When William the Conqueror was in England these banquets usually took place at Gloucester Castle at Christmas and Winchester Castle at Easter.

A thirteenth-century writer called Bartholomew the Englishman described the etiquette of the hall on a day of grand banqueting. The meal began with the display of meats and the summoning of the guests. Hands were carefully washed and guests sat down in the appropriate places. Several courses of meat were eaten and wine was drunk. Entertainers played lutes and harps. The meal concluded with a final course of fruit and spices. Afterwards, the diners continued

ABOVE *A late thirteenth-century painted glass beaker from Launceston Castle in Cornwall – possibly Venetian in origin. A precious vessel such as this would have been used in the great hall*

ABOVE *A king dines in great state, while his musicians play. The ritual of dining was an expression of the hierarchy of the castle household*

BELOW *A simple instrument, sometimes known as a 'Jew's harp', found at Castle Rising Castle in Norfolk*

LEFT *Monarchs and nobles were the chief patrons of musicians such as these, depicted in a thirteenth-century manuscript*

for feasting and merry-making was Christmas. In some surviving household accounts preparations for the Christmas festivities start as early as October. The anonymous poem *Sir Gawain and the Green Knight*, dating from the fourteenth century, gives a vivid, if imaginary, picture of a great castle at Christmas time. The poet described how the household spent the holiday period in festive mood:

> For fifteen days the feasting there was
> full in like measure
> With all the meat and merry-making
> men could devise,
> Gladly ringing glee, glorious to hear,
> A noble din by day, dancing at night!
> All was happiness in the height in halls
> and chambers
> For lords and their ladies, delectable joy.

Hospitality and entertainment were accompanied by substantial consumption of alcohol. While humbler people drank beer and cider, the drink of the rich and the powerful was imported French wine. The trade in wine was a major component of the business of the ports of London, Southampton and Bristol. The butler was the household officer responsible for purchasing, storing and serving wine. Wine was transported in large casks or 'tuns', each of which contained 252 gallons. In one week in August 1265 the garrison at Dover Castle drank three-quarters of a tun of wine.

The tradition of the lord or lady dining with the whole household had begun to decline by the middle of the fourteenth century. By the late Middle Ages it was much more common for the lord and lady normally to dine in private. The hall would still be used on feast-days, or when important visitors were to be entertained. In a famous passage written in the fourteenth century the poet William Langland condemned the tendency to private dining:

ABOVE *An oven built into the buttresses of the keep at Dunstanburgh Castle, Northumberland*

BELOW *A decorated copper jug that was once the property of Richard II. It was discovered in a palace in the Gold Coast (now Ghana) in 1895*

drinking until 'The grace is said, and guests thank the lord. Then, for gladness and comfort, drink is brought yet again.'

Medieval people often had a quirky sense of humour and this might be demonstrated during a banquet. At a feast in 1172 Henry, the heir to the throne, whimsically ordered everyone, except himself, whose name was not William to leave the hall. This still left many revellers because William was such a common name!

The level of feasting depended on the Church calendar. Accounts show that abstinence from meat was strictly adhered to during Lent. Almost every surviving set of household accounts also refers to the strict observance of a meat-free diet on Fridays. Sunday, by contrast, was a day of celebration and unusual dishes, such as heron, dolphin and peacock. In the Middle Ages, as today, the single most important period

> Woe is in the hall each day
> in the week
> There the lord and lady
> like not to sit
> Now every rich man
> eats by himself
> In a private parlour to be
> rid of poor men
> Or in a chamber with a
> chimney
> And leaves the great hall.

19

THE HUNT

ABOVE *A lord emerging from a castle or citadel to go hawking. Hunting was an extremely popular pastime among the medieval monarchy and nobility*

The single most popular outdoor pastime for medieval royalty and nobility was hunting. There was a close connection between castles and hunting. Some castles, such as Pickering in Yorkshire, owed their popularity with royalty almost entirely to the quality of the nearby hunting. The tendency for the royal family to stay at Windsor, rather than in London, was influenced by Windsor's proximity to good hunting territory. When Edward III redeveloped Windsor in the fourteenth century, he established a series of satellite houses in the adjacent forest, so that wherever the chase took him there was always a nearby place for him to sleep and eat. Skilled huntsmen were prized members of the household and were well paid. Edward II's huntsman, William Twici, wrote a short book on the subject called *The Art of Hunting*. He was paid the substantial sum of 7½ pence a day. Many kings were addicted to hunting and spent every available moment on the chase. Henry II, for example, channelled much of his very considerable energy into hunting. Gerald of Wales described his passionate approach to the activity thus: 'He was addicted to hunting beyond measure: at crack of dawn he was off on horseback, traversing wastelands, penetrating forests and climbing the mountain tops, and so he passed his restless days.' A contemporary of Henry II described the therapeutic quality of hunting for those involved in the stresses and strains of high politics:

> In the forests are the privy places of kings and their great delight. Thither they go for hunting, and having laid aside their cares, to enjoy a little quiet. There, away from the continuous business and incessant turmoil of the court, they may for a little time breathe in the gracious freedom of nature. And that is why those who despoil it are subject to the royal censure alone.
> *(Richard FitzNigel writing in the 1170s)*

The most common form of hunting was with hounds. Hawking was also popular. The nature of the animals hunted was determined by social status. Anyone could hunt hares and rabbits.

ABOVE *William Rufus shown with an arrow through his heart. He died while out hunting*

LEFT *Deerhounds and greyhounds are being used during this stag hunt*

Crown through fines. Contemporaries often complained about the strictness of the law. Alan de Neville, Henry II's chief forester, was described in highly abusive terms by the chronicler of Battle Abbey in Sussex:

> By the power with which he was endowed, he most evilly vexed the various provinces throughout England with countless and unaccustomed persecutions. And since he feared neither God nor man, he spared no man of rank whether ecclesiastics or laymen. This Alan so long as he lived enriched the royal treasury, and to please an earthly king did not fear to offend the king of Heaven.

Those who fell foul of forest law could be dealt with brutally. Objections to its harshness led to the issuing of the Charter of the Forest in 1217, which removed some if its more extreme penalties. It declared, for example, that no-one should lose 'life or limb' as a result of a poaching offence. In addition, extensions of the royal forest made since the accession of Henry II were ordered to be undone.

One of the greatest of the forests created by William the Conqueror was the New Forest in Hampshire. This was conveniently located for royal visits to the castle at Winchester. The Conqueror's son, William Rufus, famously died in the New Forest as a result of a hunting accident: on 1 August 1100 Walter Tirel, one of his courtiers, accidentally killed him with an arrow intended for a stag. One chronicler saw this death as divine judgement on the harshness of the forest policy of William the Conqueror, and, in particular, the creation of the New Forest:

> Nor can it be wondered that Almighty power and vengeance should have been thus displayed. For in former times this tract of land was thickly planted with churches and with inhabitants who were worshippers of God. By command of King William the elder the people were expelled, the houses half ruined, the churches pulled down, and the land made an habitation for wild beasts only; and hence, as it is believed, arose this mischance. (*Florence of Worcester*)

Medieval kings and nobles did not hunt foxes because they were thought of as vermin and, as such, not worthy of the chase. In the royal forests, certain wild animals could only be hunted by the king or those with his warrant. These so-called 'beasts of the chase' were red, fallow and roe deer, and wild boar. Great nobles often built 'parks' near their principal castles and houses – these were large fenced enclosures built to retain the beasts of the chase.

The royal forest was not simply an area of wood and scrub solely dedicated to the king's hunting. Indeed some distant forests, such as Delamere in Cheshire and Amounderness in Lancashire, were rarely visited by royalty. Like all forests, however, they were a valuable economic resource. Venison from the forests was sent to garrisons at royal castles. Timber was also provided for building work on castles and other sites.

Forest areas included villages and cultivated land. However, the forest was subject to its own special legal system, the 'forest law'. In addition to poaching, offences against forest law included:

+ gathering timber and firewood without permission;
+ driving carts off the highway;
+ allowing pigs to forage without permission;
+ possessing dogs whose claws had not been trimmed.

The chief forester had oversight of all the forests and forest law, and reported directly to the king. Forest law generated large sums of money for the

UNEASY LIES THE HEAD

CENTRE *A melancholy royal prisoner in a castle. This manuscript depicts the imprisonment of Richard the Lionheart in Germany*

The lives of the noble and royal occupants of castles were not all, or even mainly, devoted to pleasure. These people were engaged in constant political manoeuvring in order to maintain their privileged position at the top of medieval society. This position was far from secure, and politics was a dangerous business. For those who lost out in the struggle for power the penalty might be the payment of a huge ransom or the loss of lands. On occasion, political misfortune could lead to death or a life of imprisonment. Castles were often the places where the battle for political power was played out and where the losers met their fate.

ABOVE *Those who lost out in the dangerous game of politics were sometimes held to ransom. Sixteen such hostages were imprisoned at Corfe Castle in the early thirteenth century*

Kings and nobles saw themselves as warriors and war as their vocation. After any period of warfare the castles of England were often used to confine prisoners taken in the conflict. These were almost exclusively prisoners of noble birth, who were held captive until a ransom was paid. The ransoms could be extremely lucrative. In 1217 Nicholas de Stuteville paid William Marshal £1500 in return for his freedom. Peter de Maulay took a number of important prisoners during the conflict of 1215–17 (see page 46). He kept sixteen of these prisoners at Corfe Castle in Dorset and by 1221 had been paid £9527 for them. The length of imprisonment depended on the speed with which the ransom negotiations could be concluded.

Imprisonment and ransom did not necessarily lead to long-standing hostility. William Marshal took Gilbert de Clare prisoner at the Battle of Lincoln in 1217 and Gilbert was briefly imprisoned at Gloucester Castle. A short while later he was not only released but married Marshal's daughter, Isabella.

While convention dictated that noble prisoners be detained temporarily and

then ransomed, a few political prisoners were considered too dangerous to be freed. Henry I had a tempestuous relationship with his older brother, Robert Curthose, the Duke of Normandy. Henry captured Robert in 1106 and kept him imprisoned in a series of British castles until his death, at Cardiff Castle, in 1134. In 1203 King John murdered his own nephew, Arthur of Brittany, because he had a rival claim to the throne. At the same time he captured Arthur's sister, Eleanor, and kept her as a life prisoner. Eleanor spent several decades captive in English castles. Long after King John's death, government records show that she was transported to Bristol Castle where she remained, from 1224 until her death in 1241.

Political prisoners were often kept in reasonably comfortable conditions but this was not always the case. King John fell out with the de Braose family of marcher lords. He ordered the lady of the family, Matilda de Braose, to hand over her sons. Matilda refused on the grounds that the king 'had wickedly murdered' his nephew Arthur and so could not be trusted. On hearing of this John was enraged and ordered the seizure of both Matilda and her eldest son, William. They were kept prisoner at Windsor in such poor conditions that they both starved to death.

The struggle between the English monarchy and the Welsh also led to the taking of political prisoners who were kept, often for decades, in royal castles. Owen, son of David ap Gruffyd, was imprisoned at Bristol Castle in 1283 after the execution of his father. Twenty years later, in about 1306, records show that he was still at Bristol and that a new wooden cage was being constructed to ensure that he did not escape:

> £14 for making a wooden cage bound with iron for the closer and more secure custody of Owen son of David son of Gruffyd in the castle prison so that the same Owen can be locked in the cage at nights.

The level of political violence increased in the later Middle Ages. A historian has calculated that between

ABOVE *A fifteenth-century illustration showing the Duke of Orleans imprisoned at the Tower of London after his capture at the Battle of Agincourt in 1415*

RIGHT *The effigy of Robert, Duke of Normandy, in Gloucester Cathedral. Robert spent the last years of his life as the prisoner of his brother, Henry I*

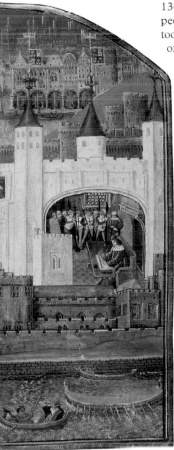

1300 and 1500 about 20 per cent of peers died violently. These deaths often took place in or near castles. The reign of Edward II illustrates both the risks of political failure and the importance of castles as the setting for the political dramas of the age. Edward had a poor relationship with many of his most powerful magnates, one of whom was Thomas, Earl of Lancaster.

In 1312 Thomas had played a central role in the capture and execution of Piers Gaveston, the favourite of Edward II. Years later, in 1322, armed conflict broke out between the king and his earl. Aware that the king had superior forces, Thomas fled north, staying en route in his castle at Pontefract. His plan was probably to flee to Scotland, via his grand new castle at Dunstanburgh, to join forces with Robert the Bruce. However, Thomas's forces were intercepted and defeated in Yorkshire by a royal army at the Battle of Boroughbridge and he was taken prisoner. A few days later Edward ordered him to be brought to Pontefract Castle. This was the king's opportunity to exact revenge for the murder of Gaveston; it was doubtless the sweeter for taking place in one of Thomas's own castles.

> The Earl of Lancaster was brought to Pontefract by the king's command, and for that night he was shut up in a certain new tower. It is said that the earl had recently built that tower, and determined that when the king was captured he should be imprisoned in it for life. On the morrow the earl was led into the hall before the justices. The earl wished to speak but the justices refused to hear him. Here was a sight indeed! To see the Earl of Lancaster, lately the scourge of the whole country, receiving judgement in his own castle and home. Then the earl was led forth from the castle and, mounted on some worthless mule, was led to the place of execution. The earl stretched forth his head as if in prayer, and the executioner cut off his head with two or three strokes.
> (*The Life of Edward II*)

The site of Thomas's execution outside Pontefract Castle became the focus of a bizarre pilgrimage when followers of the dead earl came to pay tribute to their leader. Thomas, Earl of Lancaster came to be seen by many as a martyr saint, prompting the following royal response:

> The king commanded Richard de Moseleye, constable of Pontefract Castle, to go in person to the place of execution of Thomas, late Earl of Lancaster, and prohibit a multitude of malefactors from praying in the memory of the said earl in contempt of the king. The said constable and his deputies were assaulted, and two of them, Richard de Godeleye and Robert de la Hawe, were killed.
> (*Government records, 1323*)

A few years later the king himself met a sorry end. In 1326 his estranged wife, Queen Isabella, and her lover, Roger Mortimer, invaded England from France. Edward panicked and attempted to flee to Ireland. He was captured at Neath Abbey in Wales by Henry, the brother of Thomas, Earl of Lancaster. The king was taken to Kenilworth Castle in Warwickshire where he was forced to abdicate. Edward was then moved from castle to castle until he arrived at Berkeley in Gloucestershire. Here, according to one chronicler, he met a gruesome death in September 1327:

> His tyrannous warders seized him on the night of 22 September as he lay sleeping in his room. There, with cushions, they held him down, suffocating him. Then they thrust a plumber's soldering iron, heated red hot, guided by a tube inserted into his bowels, and thus they burned his innards and his vital organs. As this brave knight was overcome, he shouted aloud so that many heard his cry, both within and without the castle.
> (*Geoffrey le Baker*)

ABOVE *The execution of Thomas of Lancaster, which took place at Thomas's own castle of Pontefract, Yorkshire in 1322*

BELOW *This fifteenth-century manuscript shows Queen Isabella meeting her lover, Roger Mortimer, in 1326. They were responsible for the murder of Edward II at Berkeley Castle a year later*

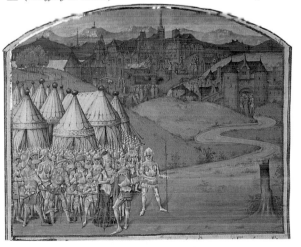

THE DEVELOPMENT OF THE CASTLE

The arrival of the Normans in Britain caused a great explosion of castle-building. Most early castles were simple structures of earth and wood, but they became more elaborate as the Middle Ages went on. The climax to the development of the castle came in the thirteenth century when Edward I built Caernarfon, and other great castles, in north Wales.

THE COMING OF THE CASTLE

ABOVE *Old Sarum, Wiltshire was an Iron Age hillfort long before the Norman Conquest. It later became the site of a medieval castle*

The Norman Conquest of 1066 marks a great watershed in the history of fortifications in Britain. There had, of course, been fortifications for many centuries before that date. Iron Age hillforts, Roman forts and Saxon town defences all provide evidence of the long history of military architecture in Britain. These earlier fortifications, however, lacked the key characteristic of the castle: the castle proper is a massively fortified private residence. Scholars disagree about when the first true castles came to Britain. Undoubtedly some were built before the Conquest, but the great explosion of castle-building came afterwards, when castles were used by the invading Normans to secure and consolidate their position. The chronicler Orderic Vitalis thought that the lack of castles in England fatally weakened the English and was a key cause of the Norman victory.

Significantly, one of William's first acts when he reached England was to build a castle at Hastings to defend his invading army. The Bayeux Tapestry depicts the construction of this castle and shows how the English were forced to help build it. William went on to establish castles in almost all towns of any significance in order to overawe his new subjects. It is clear from the Domesday Book of 1086 that in several towns large numbers of houses were demolished to create a space for the new Norman castle. The castle at Norwich, for example, required the destruction of about 100 houses; in Lincoln no fewer than 166 houses were demolished. In addition to the royal castles, William's barons built their own castles to secure control of the lands awarded to them by the Conqueror. Most of the great nobles held land in different parts of England and they constructed more than one castle.

After the Conquest castles dominated much of English life:

- ❖ they overlooked the daily activities of ordinary people in most major towns and cities;
- ❖ royal castles were centres from which the central government exercised its authority;
- ❖ baronial castles were symbols of lordly power and provided the administrative headquarters for many great landed estates.

Most early Norman castles were of the 'motte-and-bailey' type and were built of earth and timber. The motte was a flat-topped mound of earth. This was the stronghold of the castle and it was fortified with a wooden palisade (or wall) and a tower. Attached to the motte was a larger enclosure, known as

ABOVE *An artist's impression of a Roman galley arriving at Portchester, Hampshire. Like Old Sarum, this early fortification – in this case a Roman fort – was later converted into a castle*

the bailey. A bridge connected the bailey to the motte. Within the bailey there were a number of timber buildings such as a hall, stables and kitchens. There were many variations on the basic design: some castles had two baileys, for example. In addition to these castles of earth and timber the Normans built, from the beginning, a small number of stone castles centred on 'great towers'. These early stone castles include Colchester, the Tower of London and Chepstow.

No written accounts survive describing in detail life in a motte-and-bailey castle in Britain. However, in 1117 a writer from Flanders described an elaborate house built on a motte in his own country:

> The ground floor contained great boxes, casks and other domestic utensils. Above were dwelling rooms and the great chamber in which the lord and his wife slept. In the inner part of the great chamber was a private room where they used to have a fire at early dawn, or in the evening, or during sickness or time of blood-letting, or for warming the children. Adjoining this was a private dormitory for waiting maids and children. In the upper storey were garret rooms, in which on the one side the sons slept, on the other, the daughters. Here also watchmen, appointed to keep guard, slept at one time or another.
> (*Lambert of Ardres*)

Rebellions by 'over-mighty' subjects began almost immediately after the Conquest and continued throughout the Middle Ages. Within a year of the Norman Conquest Eustace of Boulogne rebelled and unsuccessfully besieged Dover Castle before fleeing the country. When the Conqueror died in 1087 there was an outbreak of castle warfare as his son, William Rufus, strove to establish his authority. Amongst the new king's chief adversaries was the Conqueror's half-brother, Bishop Odo of Bayeux, who established his head-quarters at Rochester Castle in Kent:

> His first contention was with his uncle, Bishop Odo of Bayeux …. Odo carried off booty of every kind to Rochester, plundering the king's revenues in Kent, and the lands of the archbishop. Bishop Geoffrey, with his nephew, depopulating Bath and Berkeley and part of Wiltshire, treasured up their spoil at Bristol. Roger Bigot at Norwich and Hugo de Grentesmesnil at Leicester, each with their own party, were plundering in their respective neighbourhoods.
> (*William of Malmesbury*)

William Rufus responded by attacking Odo's castles at Rochester, Tunbridge and Pevensey. Odo was captured, escaped, recaptured and finally forced to leave the country, together with the rebellious Bishop of Durham. After this the rebellion collapsed.

ABOVE *Odo, the brother of William the Conqueror, portrayed in the Bayeux Tapestry. Odo used Rochester Castle as a base when rebelling against William Rufus*

BELOW *This scene from the Bayeux Tapestry shows Dinan Castle in Normandy, a typical motte-and-bailey castle*

ABOVE *A fourteenth-century stone corbel from Brougham Castle, Cumbria*

THE AGE OF STONE

RIGHT *At Restormel Castle in Cornwall a later stone shell-keep is built on top of the earlier earth motte*

Castle-building in the twelfth century was characterised by a move from timber to stone fortifications. The century also witnessed the widespread building of great stone towers, or 'keeps' as they later became known. The contemporary name for the keep was 'donjon', a word that is derived from the Latin 'dominium' meaning lordship. Clearly, these towers were seen as symbols of the authority of the ruling class.

In some castles the earth motte was retained and the wooden palisade that

had topped the motte was replaced by a new circular stone wall. Structures of this type are known as shell-keeps. Surviving shell-keeps can be seen at Totnes in Devon and Launceston and Restormel in Cornwall. While a shell-keep was superior to a timber palisade, the earth motte was not usually capable of supporting a larger stone building and in most places the motte was abandoned in favour of a great rectangular stone tower built at ground level. These keeps derived their strength from their sheer size. The height of the keep was such that it could not easily be taken by storm. The walls were so massive that the siege engines of the time could not smash them down. Entry to a keep was at first- or second-floor level and the staircase was enclosed within a projecting 'forebuilding' which made it more difficult for the attackers to break in.

The earliest stone keeps follow a rectangular ground plan. Massive rectangular keeps were built at Colchester and the Tower of London in the eleventh century, probably during the reign of William the Conqueror. One of the greatest and latest of all the rectangular keeps was that built at

Dover between 1180 and 1190. This huge structure had walls 20 feet thick. Inside it contained two elaborate suites of rooms and two chapels.

By the time of the construction of the keep at Dover, military architects had begun to explore alternatives to the rectangular design. Despite their strength, rectangular keeps were vulnerable to attack. The corner angles provided a blind-spot for defenders. Teams of highly skilled and daring miners developed techniques for weakening the walls by digging cavities

under the corner angles, setting fire to wood placed in these cavities, and thereby causing the collapse of a large section of wall.

The late twelfth and early thirteenth centuries witnessed the emergence of circular or polygonal keeps. One of the earliest of these is the polygonal keep at Orford in Suffolk, which dates from around 1170 (before the construction of the rectangular keep at Dover). Important circular keeps can be seen at the castles at Conisbrough (Yorkshire), Pembroke (Wales) and Barnard Castle (Durham). These circular and polygonal keeps were designed with great ingenuity. At Conisborough, for example, a dovecote, an oven and water tanks were all concealed in the hollow buttresses of the keep. In the keep itself were a well, storage rooms, a chapel and some well-appointed residential accommodation.

In the early thirteenth century, while a few circular keeps continued to be built, most castle designers abandoned entirely the use of a single strong keep and put greater reliance on the development of powerful perimeter or 'curtain' walls. The curtain walls were punctuated by projecting towers, from

ABOVE LEFT *The keep at Dover was one of the last and grandest of the massive rectangular 'great towers'*

ABOVE *Ingenious castle designers experimented with polygonal keeps, such as this one at Orford*

ABOVE *Dover was trans-
formed into a concentric
castle during the thirteenth
century*

which archers and crossbow-men could
mow down the attacking force. The
weakest point in a curtain wall was the
entrance or gateway. Castle designers
responded to this by developing an
elaborate gatehouse, typically made up
of two flanking towers linked together
into one structure. This new emphasis
on the gatehouse had the effect of
turning the most vulnerable aspect of
the defensive system into its strongest
point. Symbolically the constable, the
man responsible for the defence of the
castle, often lived in the gatehouse.
Beyond the gatehouse an outlying
fortification, known as a barbican, was
sometimes developed to add further
strength to the gatehouse. When in
1225 Ranulf, Earl of Chester built a
new castle for himself at Beeston,
Cheshire, he omitted a keep entirely
and relied on curtain walls and gatehouses to ensure the castle's security.

During the thirteenth century further
defensive elements were introduced.
At some castles a second perimeter
wall was added: these are known as
'concentric castles'. The height of the
exterior wall was lower than that of the
inner wall allowing defenders on both
walls to fire at attackers. The area

between the two walls (the outer ward)
constituted a killing-ground in which
attackers could easily be trapped and
destroyed. Thirteenth-century castle
designers also began to make more
extensive use of water defences as
a response to attack by mining.

The most up-to-date thinking of
thirteenth-century castle designers can
be seen in the great baronial castle of
Caerphilly in Wales. This was begun
in 1271 by 'Red Gilbert' de Clare.
It comprises concentric curtain walls,
with a strong inner wall that incorpo-
rates four great 'drum towers', and two
great gatehouses at the east and west
ends of the castle. The fortifications
are surrounded by an enormous lake
formed by damming two local streams.

BELOW *The builder of
Caerphilly Castle was 'Red
Gilbert' de Clare. His Welsh
castle was one of the grandest
baronial castles of the
Middle Ages*

FAR RIGHT *Caerphilly,
a concentric castle with
elaborate water defences*

CASTLES AND THE CELTIC LANDS

ABOVE *Llewelyn the Last was killed in battle in 1282. His death, portrayed above, was followed by Edward I's great campaign of castle-building in north Wales*

Castles were further developed in response to troubled relations with the neighbouring peoples of Wales, Scotland and Ireland. The relationship between the Normans and the Welsh in particular centred on the building of castles. All three Celtic countries themselves adopted the use of the castle in some shape or form.

After the Battle of Hastings William the Conqueror established three powerful earldoms along the frontier with Wales (the 'marches'), each controlled from a central castle: Chester, Shrewsbury and Hereford. Other so-called marcher lords also established themselves in the area, and the Normans soon began to extend their power and influence into Wales proper. In the late eleventh and early twelfth centuries they seized much of coastal south Wales and established a series of castles there. In about 1090 Robert FitzHamo invaded the Vale of Glamorgan and set up his headquarters at Cardiff, where he built a castle in the ruins of a Roman fort. In 1106 Henry de Newburgh invaded Gower by sea and built himself a castle at Swansea. More adventurers invaded Pembroke and built castles to control their newly won lands.

The far north of England was a difficult area to control and the border was disputed with the kings of Scotland. In 1080 William the Conqueror established 'New Castle' on the Tyne as an outpost of English royal authority. William Rufus pushed further north and west with the establishment of key castles at Carlisle and Norham on the Tweed. Norman adventurers also established themselves in the Scottish lowlands. In response the Scottish royal family itself adopted the use of the castle.

In 1170 the Norman baron known as Richard FitzGilbert de Clare, or 'Strongbow', invaded Ireland. He was followed by many other Anglo-Norman families, who built castles for themselves throughout the island.

During the second half of the twelfth century there was a revival of Welsh power, centred on the three principalities of Deheubarth, Gwynedd and Powys. Like their Scottish counterparts, the Welsh princes adopted the idea of the castle. They captured and occupied a number of Norman castles and built others of their own. The greatest of the twelfth-century Welsh princes was Rhys ap Gruffyd. His headquarters was the castle of Dinefwr. By the time of his death in 1197 he had succeeded in reversing the Anglo-Norman advance into south-west Wales.

Carlisle Castle was seized by David I of Scotland during the reign of King Stephen. David completed the building of the stone keep, obviously intending to keep the castle permanently; he died there in 1153. In 1157, however, Henry II regained control of Carlisle and the surrounding territory, and this was the scene of continuing conflict between the Scottish and English monarchs in the years that followed.

BELOW. *Prisoners and animals being driven away by soldiers. Hostages were often held in castles*

ABOVE *Castles played a key role in border warfare during the Middle Ages. The Norman invasion of Wales was fiercely contested by the Welsh princes Rhys ap Gruffyd and Llewelyn the Great*

RIGHT *Norman warriors from the Bayeux Tapestry. Having conquered England, the Normans soon turned their attention to the other parts of the British Isles*

In 1173 King William the Lion of Scotland invaded northern England claiming authority over 'the whole of Northumbria as far as the Tyne'. This attack ended in disaster when William was taken prisoner while besieging Alnwick Castle. He was kept captive for two years and only released when he signed a humiliating treaty with Henry II, pledging future loyalty to Henry 'as his liege lord':

ABOVE *A fourteenth-century illustration of a castle besieged. While his colleagues try to scale the walls, one attacker sets fire to the castle's gate. Inside there is a woman defender on the battlements*

In order that this treaty and pact may be faithfully kept by the king of the Scots and his heirs, the king of the Scots has delivered to the lord king Henry the castles of Roxburgh, Berwick, Jedburgh, Edinburgh and Stirling, to be held by the lord king Henry at his pleasure. And the king of the Scots shall pay for the garrison of these castles out of his own revenue at the pleasure of the lord king Henry
(*Treaty of Falaise 1175*)

Hostages were often taken in the wars with the Scots and the Welsh, and were then kept captive in English castles. King John notoriously executed a large group of Welsh hostages at Nottingham Castle in 1212:

About this time the Welsh burst fiercely forth from their hiding places, and took some of the English king's castles, decapitating all they found in them, knights and soldiers alike. When these events became known to the English king he was very indignant.

On his arriving with his army at Nottingham, before he either ate or drank, he ordered twenty-eight youths, whom he had received the year before as hostages from the Welsh, to be hung on the gibbet in revenge.
(*Roger of Wendover*)

The princes of the northern Welsh principality of Gwynedd dominated Welsh politics in the thirteenth century. Their power reached its pinnacle in 1267, during the reign of Llewelyn ap Iorwerth (also known as Llewelyn the Great), to whom Henry III granted the title Prince of Wales. Welsh ascendancy was reversed decisively by Henry's successor Edward I. The Welsh were defeated in the wars of 1276–77 and 1282–83 and a great campaign of castle-building was initiated in order to secure the conquest of north Wales (see page 30).

Edward I also attempted to destroy Scotland as an independent force. By comparison with his Welsh campaign, however, he was much less successful and his plan to build a series of new castles in Scotland came to nothing. English power over Scotland was dealt a further blow during the reign of his son, Edward II (1307–27).

The Scottish king Robert the Bruce won a decisive victory at Bannockburn, near Stirling Castle, in 1314. Unlike Wales, Scotland was able to retain its separate political identity for the rest of the Middle Ages.

The Anglo-Norman rulers of Ireland gradually intermarried with the Irish people and adopted their language. By the late Middle Ages English political control of Ireland had largely disappeared, apart from the area known as the Pale, centred on Dublin and its castle.

ABOVE *A scene from the siege of Carlisle in 1315. Carlisle Castle was often a focus of Anglo-Scottish conflict*

BELOW *Norham Castle, Northumberland was built as part of the attempt to extend Norman control in the north of England*

BOTTOM *There was sporadic border warfare between the English and Scots throughout the Middle Ages*

THE CASTLE AT ITS PEAK

ABOVE *A king and his architect. A skilled military architect was highly prized and could command a good salary*

BELOW *Caernarfon, built on an ancient site, combined majestic strength and symbolic significance*

The castles built by Edward I in north Wales in the late thirteenth century are generally considered to be the finest examples of medieval military architecture in Britain. They were part of a deliberate plan to impose permanent English rule over Wales following the defeat of the princes of north Wales. The Edwardian castles represent a staggering investment of money and other resources. In all Edward was responsible for a total of eight new castles in Wales and he spent £80,000 on them from 1277 to 1304. In addition he redeveloped the Tower of London at a cost of over £20,000 between 1275 and 1285. In Wales Edward and his architect, Master James of St George (see page 32), were responsible for some of the great masterpieces of medieval castle design.

Taken together, the Edwardian castles contain a number of key design elements:

* the castles had no keep and relied on a strong curtain wall, with regularly placed wall towers;
* there were two distinct lines of defence, either in the form of concentric curtain walls or two separate defensible enclosures or 'wards';
* the gatehouse played an important part in the castle's defensive capacity;
* castles were situated when possible close to the coast and, in the event of a siege, could be supplied by ship;
* the castle defences were often integrated with existing town walls, or new towns were established at the same time as a new castle was built.

These principles were in keeping with the latest international thinking on castle design. Edward's gifted military architect, Master James of St George, was foreign and had worked for several years in Savoy before coming to Britain. Edward appears to have 'head-hunted' him after a visit to his cousin, the Count of Savoy, in 1273. The king clearly took a keen personal interest in the progress of his castles. Late in his life he went so far as to push a symbolic wheel-barrow of earth during the building of the ramparts at Berwick!

Edward was involved in extensive repair and building work at a large number of castles in England, Scotland and Wales. However, the four greatest of the Edwardian castles are the Welsh castles of Conwy, Harlech, Beaumaris and Caernarfon. At each of them Master James of St George applied the principles of contemporary castle design to a particular site and produced a distinct and distinguished solution. Edward was sensitive to symbolism and Conwy was an attractive site because it required the demolition of the Cistercian abbey in which the Welsh prince, Llewelyn the Great, was buried. The castle was located on a long spine of rock, which made a concentric design impossible. Instead the designer placed two wards side by side with a dividing wall as large as the external wall, so that the two parts of the castle could be separately defended. A new walled town was built at the same time and the defences of the town are integrated with the castle itself. The surviving town walls are remarkably intact. Within the towers of the inner ward Master James provided private apartments and a beautiful chapel for the king. The outer ward enclosed stables, kitchens and the great hall, and provided tower accommodation for the constable. Conwy Castle and town were constructed at great speed and the whole design was virtually complete by 1287.

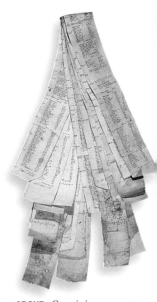

ABOVE *Surviving accounts provide a vivid picture of the building of the great castles of north Wales. These rolls relate to expenses incurred at Caernarfon*

Harlech, like Conwy, was built near the sea at a magnificent site on an outcrop of rock. This time the nature of the site did lend itself to a concentric design. It was begun in 1283 and largely finished by 1290. In that year Master James was appointed constable. The greatest strength of Harlech Castle lies in the magnificent inner ward with its four great drum towers and its majestic gatehouse. The gatehouse contains the best accommodation and would presumably have housed both visiting royalty and the distinguished constable of the castle.

The last of the great Edwardian castles was Beaumaris, on Anglesey. Like Harlech it followed a concentric design but, unlike Harlech, it was built on flat, marshy land.

There is no doubt that Caernarfon was conceived by its builders as the greatest of all the Edwardian castles. It was established as the administrative centre for the government of newly-conquered north Wales. Like Conwy

the setting was not suitable for a concentric design and two wards were placed side by side. The choice of Caernarfon as a site was full of symbolism. It was the ancient capital of the principality of Gwynedd, and had also once been a Roman settlement called *Segontium*. According to Welsh tradition it was the burial place of the Roman emperor Magnus Maximus. It was, therefore, a fitting place for the new emperor of Britain to demonstrate his power and glory. The design of the castle is full of imperialistic symbols. The unusual polygonal towers and banded masonry are, almost certainly, derived from the defences of Emperor Theodosius in Constantinople, the so-called Second Rome. Its greatest tower, the Eagle Tower, had three turrets, each capped with a stone carving of that most imperious of birds. Edward's wife Queen Eleanor was brought to Caernarfon Castle in April 1284 so that the heir to the throne would be born there.

ABOVE *Edward I enters London as a new king. During his reign castle design in Britain reached its climax*

BELOW *Harlech Castle as it might have appeared in about 1325. Like so many of the Edwardian castles it was built on a coastal site*

EDWARD'S MASTER MASON

The greatest architects of the Middle Ages were usually masons by training. One such was Master James of St George, the chief architect of the castles of Edward I.

The career of James of St George illustrates the cosmopolitan character of medieval life. In the summer of 1273 Edward I was the guest of his cousin Count Philip of Savoy. He stayed at the castle of St Georges, which was then being rebuilt, and it was almost certainly on this occasion that he came across the great military architect. (James was probably responsible for a series of castles in the region, but it was with the castle of St Georges that his name later became permanently linked in England.) The last mention of James in the archives of Savoy is in 1275. He appears in the English records in the spring of 1278 when he travelled to Wales 'to ordain [direct] the works of the castles there'. Several other craftsmen from Savoy appear to have accompanied James to Wales. Philip the Carpenter, for example, had worked with James in Savoy and in 1286 was the main carpenter responsible for the roofing of Flint Castle. Over ten years later he appears again, as a property-owner in the town of Caernarfon.

The first castles with which James was associated were Flint, Rhuddlan, Builth and Aberystwyth. He was eventually appointed as 'Master of the King's Works in Wales'. His work was evidently appreciated because from 1283 he was paid the unprecedented sum of 3 shillings a day. Shortly afterwards his wife Ambrosia was promised a very large pension of 1 shilling and sixpence a day in the event of his death. In the 1280s he appears to have been based for a number of years at Conwy, although we know that he also travelled widely. Further favours were received by James: in 1290 he became constable of Harlech Castle. This entitled him to live in some comfort at the new castle. In 1295 he was granted the valuable manor of Mostyn, worth over £25 a year. During the mid-1290s his chief preoccupation was the construction of a new castle on Anglesey at Beaumaris. After 1298, however, his attention turned to the king's military campaign in Scotland, and in 1304 he was the chief engineer responsible for the siege of Stirling. We know that James also visited Gascony in company with the king and his army. He died in about 1309.

Some of the trials involved in castle-building are evident in the correspondence between James and the government in London in 1296. The building of Beaumaris Castle on Anglesey followed a Welsh rebellion on the island in September 1294. The king's close friend Roger de Pulesdon, sheriff of Anglesey, was taken by the rebels and hanged. Edward reacted swiftly and vigorously to the uprising. Despite the fact that winter was setting in he ordered an immediate campaign to re-take the island. By the spring of 1295 Anglesey had been recaptured and documents show that James was on the island in April of that year beginning work on the new castle. An existing settlement was destroyed and the Welsh inhabitants were moved to a new village twelve miles away.

Work at Beaumaris proceeded rapidly and in February 1296 James sent a written report to London. The letter shows how the royal mason needed to be a fine administrator and man-manager as well as a distinguished architect. It also gives some sense of the enormous scale of the Edwardian castle-building project:

Sirs,
As our lord the king has commanded us to let you have a clear picture of all aspects of the state of the works at Beaumaris, we write to inform you that the work we are doing is very costly and we need a great deal of money. You should know:
1. That we have kept on masons, stone cutters, quarrymen and minor workmen all through the winter, and are still employing them, for making mortar and breaking up stone for lime; we have had carts bringing stone to the site and bringing timber for erecting the buildings in which we are all now living inside the castle; we also have 1000 carpenters, smiths, plasterers and navvies, quite apart from a mounted garrison of ten men, twenty crossbow-men and 100 infantry.
2. That when this letter was written we were short of £500, for both the workmen and garrison. The men's pay has been and still is very much in arrears, and we are having the greatest

difficulty in keeping them because they simply have nothing to live on.
3. That if our lord the king wants the work to be finished as quickly as it should be, we could not make do with less than £250 a week throughout the season.

Master James went on to explain that some of the castle stood at 28 feet high and that even at its lowest point its walls were 20 feet high. He informed the government that work had begun on ten outer towers and four inner towers. Gateways were in place and each one was locked every night. He obviously took considerable pride in this achievement, declaring: 'So much we have been able to do in spite of all the Welshmen.' Master James appears to have had a fairly jaundiced view of his Welsh foe. The letter speculates on the possibility of renewed Welsh rebellion: 'As to how things are in the land of Wales, we still cannot be any too sure. But, as you well know, Welshmen are Welshmen.' The great architect justified his financial demands by listing his huge manpower requirements:

In case you should wonder where so much money could go in a week, we would have you know that we have needed – and shall continue to need – 400 masons, both cutters and layers, together with 2000 minor workmen, 100 carts, 60 wagons, and 30 boats bringing stone and sea-coal; 200 quarrymen; 30 smiths; and carpenters. All this takes no account of the garrison, nor of purchases of materials, of which there will have to be a great quantity.

The letter concludes dramatically. 'P.S. For God's sake be quick with the money; otherwise everything done up to now will have been of no avail.' It seems that, despite this desperate plea, the government was not able to supply James with the money he requested. Instead of £250 a week, he received only £742 during the whole of the 1296 building season. Master James of St George did not live to see the completion of Beaumaris. The work continued for many years but his designs were never finished. Building at the castle finally came to an end in 1330, long after the death of its architect.

BELOW *The building of Beaumaris was fraught with problems for James*

ABOVE *We have no picture of James, and many of the castle architects of the Middle Ages are anonymous. This carving shows Henry Yevele, a distinguished fourteenth-century architect*

ABOVE *As today, medieval building sites were busy places*

BUILDING A CASTLE

ABOVE *The Bayeux Tapestry shows Normans overseeing the English as they carry out forced labour on the new castles*

The construction of a simple motte-and-bailey castle in the decades after the Conquest was, undoubtedly, a much more straight-forward enterprise than the building of an elaborate stone castle later in the Middle Ages. A very small motte-and-bailey castle could be built by fifty people, working ten hours a day, over a period of eighty working days. A large castle would take about three times this level of effort. Some of the Conqueror's castles were created in a few days. Chronicles describe how castles at Dover and York were completed in eight days. Two centuries later, the time and effort put into the building of Edward I's castle at Caernarfon was incomparably greater. Here, the huge sum of £27,000 was spent and work continued for nearly fifty years. Despite this tremendous investment the castle was never completed.

The earliest castles were not only quicker to build than later castles, they involved a simple design and required an unsophisticated workforce. As castles became more commonly built of stone, and as the standard of accommodation rose, there was a need for increasingly skilled architects and specialist crafts-men. In stone-built castles the master mason played a central role, typically both designing the castle and coordinating the work of labourers and craftsmen. Skilled master masons were sought after and were very well paid. At the great baronial castle of Dunstanburgh in Northumberland in the early fourteenth century the architect was a mason named Master Elias. His patron was Thomas, Earl of Lancaster, the richest magnate in England. Elias was paid the phenomenal sum of £280 for his work on the castle.

After the master mason and his team of skilled stonemasons, the most sig-nificant craftsmen were the carpenters. These woodworkers often combined work on castle construction with involvement in the design and building of the siege engines that were used to attack enemy castles.

Although builders were usually better paid than many other workers, there were times of intense castle-building when there was a shortage of both skilled and unskilled labour. In these circumstances the government forced people to contribute to the royal castle-building programme. When Edward I built his great Welsh castles, thousands of labourers were forced to go to Wales from all over England. Some resisted impressment and armed guards were needed to escort them to the work.

After the Black Death of the mid-fourteenth century, building workers frequently deserted their posts because the reduction in the population meant they could command better wages elsewhere. Edward III had great difficulty in obtaining labour for his rebuilding of Windsor. The sheriff of Yorkshire ordered that masons sent from Yorkshire to Windsor be forced to wear distinctive red clothes so that they could be identified if they attempted to flee on the journey south. The scale of the work at Windsor threatened to under-mine the building schemes of contemporary nobles and churchmen:

> Almost all the masons and carpenters throughout England were brought to Windsor Castle, so that hardly anyone else could have any good mason or carpenter, except in secret. (Polychronicon, *a fourteenth-century chronicle history*)

ABOVE *In this German example of castle-building, a crane, powered by a treadmill, is used in the construction of a tower*

Rival patrons eventually foiled the attempt to force building workers to go to Windsor by offering higher wages. In 1361 and 1362 Edward was forced to issue proclamations stating new penalties for workers who abandoned the king's works:

> For excessive gain and gifts almost all the masons and craftsmen hired for the king's works in his castles have secretly withdrawn, and are retained with religious persons and other masters, to the king's hurt and hindrance of his works, whereat he is moved to anger. (*Edward III, 1362*)

The building season lasted through the spring and summer months. During the winter much building work stopped and most workers were laid off. The records from Harlech Castle in 1286 give a very accurate picture of

BELOW *Dunstanburgh Castle. The architect, Master Elias, was extremely well paid*

the seasonal nature of the work. In January only sixty-two people were on the pay-roll; by July the number of workers had risen to 944. Occasionally, if the work was considered urgent, building might continue through the winter. In autumn 1243 the pious Henry III was keen that work on the chapel of St Edward at Windsor should be completed as soon as possible. He wrote from France, giving instructions that indicate the high quality of craftsmanship that was expected in a thirteenth-century royal castle:

> Cause work to go on both in winter and in summer until the king's chapel of Windsor is finished, and have a high wooden roof made after the manner of the new work at Lichfield, so that it may appear to be stonework, with good wainscoting and painting, and cause the chapel to be covered with lead, and have four gilt images made in the said chapel, and placed in those places in which the king had previously arranged for such images to be placed, and a stone tower at the front of the said chapel, in which may be hung three or four bells.

Despite the urgency of Henry's message, the work at Windsor was not completed for several years. Government records show that a full five years later painters were still at work on the interior decoration of the chapel and the chaplains were not able to undertake their duties until 1249.

The work of the medieval builders was sometimes flawed and there were many instances of building collapses and resulting casualties. William Rishanger, a monk of St Albans, described how Prince Edward – the future King Edward I – narrowly escaped death as a young man:

> He was famed as one who enjoyed the protection of the Lord of Heaven. For example, as a boy, he was once in the middle of a game of chess with one of his knights in a vaulted room when suddenly, for no apparent reason, he got up and walked away. Seconds later a massive stone, which would have crushed completely anyone who happened to be underneath it, fell from the roof on to the very spot where he had been sitting. He attributed this miraculous escape to the Blessed Virgin of Walsingham, for whom he felt particular veneration ever afterwards.

THE CASTLE IN WAR AND PEACE

*Castles were, for much of the time, peaceful places.
They were centres for a great variety of activities: national and
local government, estate management, chivalric display and the
administration of law and order. Occasionally, during periods
of civil and national war, castles were besieged.
While the attackers used siege-engines and miners to destroy
castle walls, deadly crossbow-men worked as snipers
from the battlements.*

FEUDALISM

ABOVE *A nobleman kneels to receive the sword of knighthood from a king. It was a great offence for a noble to be disloyal to his feudal overlord*

Castles in war and peace operated within the feudal system. After the Conquest William claimed all the land of England as his. He held on to about twenty per cent of the land and gave the use of the remainder to a small number of barons and leading churchmen. These men were known as his tenants-in-chief. In return for their lands – or fiefs – the tenants-in-chief promised to provide knights for the king's wars and for the garrisoning of the king's castles. The knights, in turn, were given the use of land by the tenants-in-chief, in return for military service. This feudal hierarchy dictated relationships at every level of medieval society.

The majority of Norman castles were built not by the king, but by his great feudal nobility. William de Warenne was typical of the barons who were established in England at the time of the Conquest and consolidated their new lands with great castle-building campaigns. He owned land and castles in Normandy and was a friend of William the Conqueror. A thirteenth-century descendant, also known as William de Warenne, recalled 'how his ancestors came with William the Bastard and conquered their lands by the sword'. William fought with the Conqueror at Hastings and was rewarded with huge landed estates across thirteen different English counties. He secured his English lands by building major castles at Lewes in Sussex, Castle Acre in Norfolk and Conisbrough in Yorkshire. These castles served as the headquarters for his scattered estates.

Like so many Norman lords William combined the life of a warrior with a fierce religious devotion. With his wife Gundreda he founded Cluniac priories at both Lewes and Castle Acre, close to their castles. Gundreda died in childbirth at Castle Acre on 27 May 1085. William de Warenne died in 1088 as a result of wounds received fighting for William Rufus against rebels at the siege of Pevensey Castle.

The link between the holding of land and military prowess was clearly expressed by the nobleman Bernard de Balliol at a meeting held at Newcastle-upon-Tyne in 1174. Bernard and other nobles were discussing the possibility of a daring attack on the Scottish king, William the Lion, near Alnwick Castle, Northumberland. Arguing against those who counselled caution, Bernard said, 'He who is not bold and resolute now does not deserve to hold a fief or anything belonging thereunto.'

In battle, there was an expectation that a vassal would defend his lord at all costs. If a man's lord lost his horse, as was common, it was assumed that a vassal would give his own mount to his lord. This act put a vassal in consider-able personal danger, and guaranteed capture in the event of defeat because heavily armoured knights could not move quickly on foot. At the Battle of Hastings William had at least two horses killed beneath him. On the first occasion a knight from Maine refused to hand over his mount and William had to drag him from his horse. On the second occasion, Eustace of Boulogne acted with feudal propriety and immediately surrendered his own horse to William.

CENTRE *The king from the famous collection of medieval chess pieces found on the Scottish island of Lewis. The rules of the game reflect the nature of the feudal system*

The greatest offences according to the feudal code were rebellion against one's lord or cowardice when fighting for him. The fear of being branded a coward was powerful. In 1216 Hubert de Burgh held the castle of Dover for the king against the besieging French force. The position appeared hopeless and Prince Louis called upon Hubert to surrender. Hubert organised a conference with the other noble members of the garrison and they unanimously refused to give in, 'lest they might be branded with treachery for a cowardly submission'.

A nobleman who failed seriously in his feudal duty to his lord could be ruined for life. If a garrison was in an impossible position during a siege and its feudal lord was absent, it would often try to obtain his permission before surrendering. Without this permission it could be accused of disloyalty. The catastrophic consequences of a moment of panic are evident in the story of Henry of Essex, a leading member of the household of Henry II, whom the king appointed as his standard-bearer. In 1157 Henry was with the king in Wales when they were ambushed. Henry panicked and fled the scene, telling all he met that the king had almost certainly been killed. In fact, the king survived the attack but afterwards Henry of Essex was tried and found guilty of treason for deserting his lord and spreading a rumour of the king's death. Henry was stripped of all his substantial wealth and ordered to spend the rest of his life in a monastery. An even worse fate awaited some of the men of Roger de Lacy in 1191. Roger remained loyal to Richard the Lionheart, who was abroad on crusade, when his brother John rose up in rebellion against him. Roger had charge of a number of castles for the king, including those

at Nottingham and Tickhill; he was incensed when he heard that, against his orders, the garrisons of these two castles had surrendered to John. Roger hanged two of the men responsible for the surrender and the bodies were left exposed on a gibbet. When the squire of one of the hanged men tried to scare the birds from his master's corpse, Roger arrested him and hanged him as well. In 1216 when John accepted the surrender of the garrison at Colchester Castle he treated the French and English prisoners differently. The French, who were not his feudal vassals, were allowed to leave honourably with their horses and weapons, while the English, who had betrayed their feudal loyalty, were placed in chains.

The keeper of a royal castle who was disloyal to his master risked not only death, but the aggravated form of execution known as hanging, drawing and quartering that was the penalty for treason. This involved the disembowelling of the victims while they were still alive. Andrew de Harcla, Earl of Carlisle, suffered such a fate. He was arrested in the hall of Carlisle Castle in 1323 and accused of conspiring with the Scottish king, Robert the Bruce, against Edward II. He met his protracted and painful end on the Gallow's Hill at Carlisle.

THE CODE OF CHIVALRY

While the feudal system controlled the relationship between a lord and his vassal, the code of chivalry governed the way in which members of the warrior class – the people who lived in castles – treated each other. The chivalric code was essentially a loose set of principles, which changed over time and was not always adhered to, but which did nonetheless exert a powerful influence on the behaviour of the nobility.

Some of the chivalric values of the great nobility are revealed in a conversation that took place at Gloucester Castle in 1216. The Earl of Chester and William Marshal were discussing who should rule the country now that King John was dead. The young king, Henry III, was only nine years old and a regent was needed. The Earl of Chester insisted that Marshal should take on this role, saying:

> You are so good a knight, so fine a man, so feared, so loved, and so wise that you are considered one of the first knights in the world. I say to you in all loyalty that you must be chosen. I will serve you, and I will carry out to the best of my ability all the tasks that you may assign to me.
> *(Biography of William Marshal)*

William Marshal had won his reputation for chivalric excellence as a warrior and as a successful competitor in the world of the tournament (see page 40). Behaviour on the battlefield and at the tournament ground was governed by a set of rules that were part of the chivalric code. A guiding principle was that it was dishonourable to attack a defenceless opponent. William the Conqueror is said to have stripped one of his followers of his belt of knighthood because he had struck King Harold on the leg as he lay on the battlefield.

Knights in combat tried to avoid slaying a knightly adversary, preferring to take him captive. This principle was made more attractive by the possibility of a large ransom being paid for his return. At the battle that took place outside Lincoln Castle in 1217 the royalist commanders, led by William Marshal, ordered their crossbow-men to shoot at the horses of their enemies rather than the riders themselves:

> At length, by means of the crossbow-men, by whose skill the horses of the barons were mown down and killed like pigs, the party of the barons was greatly weakened. For when the horses fell to earth, slain, their riders were taken prisoners as there was no one to rescue them. *(Roger of Wendover)*

While chivalry entailed respect for other members of the knightly class, it offered little protection for the great majority of the population. William Marshal, although generally regarded as a paragon of chivalry, was apparently unconcerned about the way his men looted the property of innocent townsfolk after the Battle of Lincoln:

> The whole city was plundered to the last farthing, and then they proceeded to rob all the churches throughout the city, breaking open all chests and cupboards with hatchets and hammers, and seizing gold and silver, cloth of all colours, women's ornaments, gold rings, goblets and precious stones. When at last they had carried off all kinds of merchandise so that nothing remained untouched in any corner of the houses, they all returned to their own lords rich men.
> *(Roger of Wendover)*

The idea that knights were members of a special caste, and followed a clear code of conduct, was reinforced by the ceremonial associated with knighthood. Young noblemen formally became knights at a special dubbing ceremony. One of the first acts of William Marshal as regent was to organise the dubbing of the nine-year-old Henry III, so that he would have the status of a knight. Earlier, in 1128, an elaborate ceremony accompanied the dubbing of Geoffrey of Anjou by Henry I:

> After bathing, Geoffrey donned a linen undergarment, a tunic of cloth of gold, silk stockings, and shoes ornamented with golden lions. A Spanish horse of wonderful beauty was provided, swifter than the flight of birds. He was then armed with a corselet of double-woven mail which no lance or javelin could pierce, and shod with iron boots; golden spurs were girded on; a shield with golden lions was

ABOVE *This fifteenth-century parade shield is decorated with a knight and his lady*

BELOW *Medieval lords talked about courtly love but the reality was sometimes very different. This fourteenth-century illustration shows a man beating his wife*

ABOVE *The top of a fourteenth-century round table is suspended from the wall in the hall of Winchester Castle. It was probably painted in Tudor times. Medieval kings saw castles as the backdrop for their chivalric rituals, which were full of references to Arthurian legend*

hung around his neck; a helmet was placed on his head gleaming with many precious stones. Thus our novice knight was armed, the future flower of knighthood, who despite his armour leapt with marvellous agility on his horse. (*Jean of Tours*)

The ritual grew more elaborate as the Middle Ages progressed. Novice knights often spent the night before the dubbing in a vigil of prayer in a church or castle chapel. During the dubbing ceremony they promised to use their power to fight evil and defend the weak. Even at the time, however, perceptive observers noticed a gulf between the theory of chivalry and the brutal reality of knightly conduct:

Young knights receive their swords from the altar and thereby they profess that they are the sons of the Church and that they have taken up the sword for the honour of the priesthood, the protection of the poor, for the punishment of malefactors, and for the liberation of the homeland. But matters are very different; for immediately they have been girt with the belt of knighthood they at once rise up against the anointed of the Lord. They despoil and rob the poor of Christ, and miserably oppress the wretched without mercy. (*Peter of Blois*)

As Peter of Blois remarked, there were distinct limitations to the application of the code of chivalry. Courtesy towards a defeated opponent was not a principle that applied to enemy infantry. In the eleventh and twelfth centuries enemy foot-soldiers were often massacred if taken prisoner. Archers and crossbow-men were frequently singled out for particularly brutal treatment. For example, John spared the majority of the garrison at Rochester after the siege of 1215, but he made an exception of some of the

crossbow-men who were hanged. The knightly class seems particularly to have resented members of the lower orders who possessed military ability. In 1263 Gloucester Castle was besieged by an army of baronial rebels. At the conclusion of the siege a carpenter who had shot dead a squire in the baronial army was forced to jump to his death from the top of the keep.

A similar double standard and class distinction also influenced the way knights treated women. The code of chivalry may have encouraged male members of the nobility to behave with respect towards women of their own class, but there is no evidence that this was extended to poor women. In one book of advice for noblemen, written in the twelfth century, the author encouraged his readers to abuse any poor country women that they desired:

If you should, by some chance, fall in love with a peasant woman, be careful to puff her up with lots of praise and then, when you find a convenient place, do not hesitate to take what you seek and to embrace her by force. For you can hardly soften their outward inflexibility unless first you use a little compulsion as a convenient cure for their shyness. (*Andreas Capellanus*)

39

THE TOURNAMENT

ABOVE *An 'aquamanile' made of copper alloy in the thirteenth century. This water dispenser was filled through the helmet and emptied through a spout on the horse's head. The armed knight is ready for combat*

Much of the code of chivalry related to behaviour between enemies on the battlefield; by extension it applied to the conduct of tournaments. The first tournaments developed in France before the twelfth century. They were a form of training for cavalry fighting and were close in spirit to full-blooded warfare. Teams of knights fought violently until one side submitted and the vanquished were taken prisoners. A chaotic clash of this kind became known as a mêlée. Participants were motivated by the glory that came with victory and the financial reward that resulted from the ransoming of prisoners. In some ways tournaments might be compared to modern spectator sports. Team members wore the same colours, their war cries were like team chants and they usually had a team leader or manager.

By the reign of Henry I the tournament had spread to Britain and the king himself participated. However, Henry II banned tournaments in England, though he allowed them to continue in some of his continental possessions. Young knights visited the continent of Europe in order to take part. One of the most successful practitioners was William Marshal, who was later made Earl of Pembroke and lord of Chepstow Castle. Between the ages of twenty-one and thirty-seven Marshal's chief preoccupation was the tournament, and his success brought him fame and fortune. Marshal became, in effect, team manager for a band of

BELOW *A fifteenth-century depiction of the court of King Arthur. The tournaments staged by Edward III at Windsor Castle were a deliberate evocation of the Arthurian world*

knights led by Henry, 'the young King', the oldest son of Henry II. As he lay dying many years later, Marshal reminisced that he had probably taken prisoner about 500 knights during the time he had spent competing in tournaments.

This was a period in which the tournament, following Henry II's ban, was beginning to regain respectability. In 1194, fearing that French knights were gaining martial superiority through their greater access to tournaments, Richard the Lionheart granted a new license for tournaments to be held in England.

Early tournaments were repeatedly condemned by the Church. Young knights continued to arrange and participate in them, however – an indication of the limited scope of the authority of the Church over the great nobility. A late twelfth-century writer, William of Newburgh, tried to explain why young men were prepared to defy the Church over tournaments:

> Although such a solemn assembly of knights is forbidden by authority under a heavy censure, yet the fervour of those youths, who in their vanity seek glory in arms and who rejoice in the fervour of kings, who desire to have expert soldiers, has treated with contempt the provisions of this ecclesiastical decree, even to this present day.

The pious and unwarlike Henry III disapproved of tournaments and on several occasions intervened in order to prevent them from taking place. Matthew Paris records how in 1248 he relented and permitted a tournament at Newbury. His description gives some sense of the importance of the tournament to young knights anxious to prove themselves as warriors:

> 1248: On Ash Wednesday a grand tournament among the knights of England, strenuously to test their military skill, was held at Newbury. Since the lord king was in favour of it, it started and ended admirably. William of Valence, half-brother of the king, a novice intent on acquiring

ABOVE *William Marshal unhorses an opponent. William achieved fame and fortune through his success on the tournament circuit*

knightly renown, took part there, advancing with audacious spirit, but his tender age and imperfect strength not allowing him to resist the impetus of hardened and warlike knights, he was prostrated and, as an initiation to knighthood, thoroughly beaten. (*Matthew Paris*)

Henry's son Edward I was a more martial figure and was better disposed towards the tournament. In 1273, shortly after he became king, Edward took part in a tournament on the continent. This account by William Rishanger of St Albans Abbey describes a violent encounter between Edward and the Count of Chalons:

The two parties rushed into combat, battering each other in a hail of sword thrusts and exerting all the strength they possessed. The count broke through Edward's formation and joined battle with him, man to man; he cast aside his sword, drew closer, and grabbed Edward round the neck, squeezing as hard as he could in an effort to drag Edward from his horse. Edward spurred his horse and pulled the count out of his saddle. This left the count hanging round Edward's neck but the prince threw him off roughly and hurled him to the ground.

The development of the tournament stimulated the growing art of heraldry.

Competitors were identified by their distinctive coats of arms. The tournament also contributed to the development of a sense of knightly identity that transcended national boundaries. Tournaments were cosmopolitan affairs, with knights competing from all over Christendom.

In the fourteenth and fifteenth centuries the tournament became a more respectable and elaborate event. Controlled one-to-one jousting gradually replaced the chaos of the mêlée. The tournament became an opportunity for a display of self-consciously chivalric ceremonial. Edward III was a great lover of the tournament and the massive redevelopment of Windsor Castle during his reign was intended to provide a splendid setting for great tournaments and other displays of chivalry (see page 56). Edward's love of the tournament was linked to his wish to emulate the heroes of Arthurian romance:

In January 1344 the king held a great tournament at Windsor and he made a great supper at which he began his Round Table. He received the oaths of certain earls and barons and knights whom he wished to be of the said Round Table and he fixed the day of holding the Round Table in the same place on the feast of the Pentecost next after. (*Adam Murimuth*)

BESIEGED!

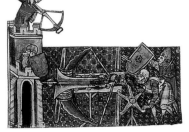

ABOVE *Besieging forces use a ballista – a large mounted crossbow which shot huge bolts*

ABOVE *The seal of the City of Rochester shows the castle and its great keep, the setting of one of the most dramatic sieges of the Middle Ages*

Warfare itself in the early Middle Ages often centred on the siege of castles. Before 1200 the advantage usually lay with the defenders. A small number of defending soldiers could successfully resist a large attacking force for a protracted period. Prolonged sieges were extremely expensive for the besieging forces. One contemporary estimated that the siege of Rochester cost King John 60,000 marks (£90,000). In addition to the financial burden a besieging army ran a high risk of mortality through disease, particularly dysentery and typhus.

The conduct of a siege was usually governed by certain conventions. Garrisons often negotiated a so-called respite from the attacking army. Under the terms of a respite the siege was lifted for a set number of days, while the defending army attempted to obtain reinforcements. If the garrison was unable to get extra help by the end of the period of the respite they agreed to surrender. Respites were attractive to attacking forces because they offered the prospect of capturing the castle without the casualties and costs involved in taking the castle by force. In granting a respite they clearly gambled on the likelihood of the defenders receiving reinforcement. In 1174 William the Lion, the Scottish king, was besieging Carlisle Castle. Robert de Vaux, the constable of the castle, asked William for a respite and the Scottish king is said to have replied, 'I have no apprehension at all about granting you a truce; you will not get any help, I know that for a fact.' William's confidence was unfounded: the garrison won the gamble when the siege was abandoned.

The medieval nobility liked to imagine that knights on horseback were the key players in warfare. This was not the case in practice. During a siege humbler fighters were often more significant. An attacking commander relied heavily upon the miners who undermined castle walls and the men who designed and used the stone-throwing machines that were used to batter castle walls.

Within the besieged castle the most dangerous soldiers were the crossbow-men who functioned as snipers. The use of the crossbow became common in the twelfth century and teams of skilled professional crossbow-men played an important part in siege warfare. Their skills were highly valued and they were paid considerably more than ordinary soldiers. Before the development of plate armour knights wore 'hauberks', coats of mail that reached to the knees and were worn over a padded tunic. Hauberks could protect their wearers from arrow fire, unless they were fired at close range. Both Henry I and Henry II were hit by arrows but unhurt. However, hauberks could do little to stop the bolt of a crossbow. Richard the Lion-heart died from a wound infection in 1199 after he had been hit by a crossbow bolt while fighting in the Crusades. A few years later, in 1216, the siege of Barnard Castle in Northumberland was abandoned when Eustace de Vesci, lord of Alnwick Castle, was killed by a defending crossbow-man. Noble warriors seem to have resented the lethal power of the humble crossbow-man. They saw the crossbow as an unchivalrous weapon. An incident that took place during the siege of Rochester in 1215 shows the power of the crossbow-man – and gives an insight into medieval views of kingship. A defending crossbow-man identified King John below and asked permission to kill him:

One day during the siege of Rochester Castle, the king was riding round it to examine the weaker parts of it, when a crossbow-man in the service of William de Albini saw him and said to his master, 'Is it your will, my lord, that I should slay the king, our bloody enemy, with this bolt which I have ready?' To this William replied, 'No, no; far be it from us, villain, to cause the death of the Lord's anointed. (*Matthew Paris*)

The garrison at Rochester was eventually forced to surrender. The crossbow-men had taken a heavy toll against the attackers and the mercy

ABOVE *Siege warfare was governed by rules and conventions. Here heralds call upon the defenders to surrender*

shown to King John was not reciprocated. John spared most of the garrison but ordered that several of the crossbow-men be hanged.

The bolts used on medieval crossbows were known as quarrels. They were wooden and tipped with iron. Most quarrels were manufactured in woodland areas, and the major royal centre of quarrel-making was St Briavels Castle, in the Forest of Dean. Royal records reveal that in 1256 the chief quarrel-maker at St Briavels was one John Malemort. He made 100 quarrels a day, or 25,000 a year. He was paid 10½ pence a day for making and 'feathering' the bolts.

Siege-engine technology developed in the early years of the thirteenth century. A more powerful and accurate machine, known as a 'trebuchet', was introduced to Britain from France. It is thought to have been brought to England by Prince Louis in 1216. The trebuchet used counter-weight technology to propel its missile. A large trebuchet could throw a stone of 300 pounds in weight a distance of over 150 metres. (Stones of this size have been excavated at Kenilworth and were probably used in the siege of Kenilworth Castle in 1266.)

The carpenters who made siege engines were often referred to as 'engineers'. Their importance is shown by King John's determination to secure the release of Ferrand the Engineer. John ordered the

release of a prisoner called Peter in exchange for Ferrand but warned that if Ferrand had been mutilated, equivalent harm would be done to Peter: 'If Ferrand be whole, let Peter be delivered whole also; but if Ferrand be lacking in any limb, Peter must first be deprived of the same limb and then delivered in exchange.' This incident also suggests that it was assumed that a skilled engineer might be mutilated if he fell into the hands of the enemy. Many siege engines were manufactured within castles. The greatest centre for their production was the Tower of London. In 1244 Girard the Carpenter is reported at work in Dover Castle, constructing a trebuchet, a catapult and a battering-ram. Almost certainly the same man occurs in the records at Carlisle Castle in 1255, where he was involved in the construction of large catapults.

ABOVE *Defenders were often at a considerable advantage over attackers, and scaling a castle wall was a perilous undertaking*

RIGHT *This early fourteenth-century manuscript illustrates a siege at the Tower of London. The attackers use a trebuchet and a scaling ladder, while the defenders hurl stones and a sniper picks off the enemy with a crossbow*

KING STEPHEN AND THE EMPRESS

ABOVE *'The empress' Matilda claimed the throne of England as the only surviving legitimate child of Henry I*

LEFT *The great hall of Castle Hedingham, Essex, built about 1140. Stephen's wife was, confusingly, also called Matilda. This was one of her favourite castles and she died here in 1152*

Warfare did not always require a foreign enemy. In times when royal authority was weak, civil war threatened to break out. Castles were used by opportunistic nobles to build a local power base by seizing control of nearby land and people.

On the death of Henry I in December 1135 there was confusion about the control of the English monarchy. The king had died without a legitimate male heir. The two contenders for the crown were his nephew, Stephen of Blois, and his daughter Matilda (known as 'the empress' because she was the widow of the German Emperor). Stephen moved quickly and decisively: he took control of London and Winchester and was crowned as king. At first his coup appeared successful but in 1138 Robert of Gloucester (the illegitimate son of Henry I) announced that he was defying the authority of Stephen and supporting the claims of his half-sister, Matilda. The empress herself landed in England in 1139. The heartland of Matilda's faction was in the West Country, including the key castles of Bristol and Gloucester. William of Malmesbury, a contemporary whose monastery was close to much of the fighting, described conditions as the country moved towards civil war:

There were many castles all over England, each defending its own district, or rather plundering it. The knights from the castles carried off both herds and flocks, sparing neither churches nor graveyards, pillaging the dwellings of the wretched countrymen to the very straw.

The warfare of Stephen's reign centred on the siege of strategically important castles. The attacking force often constructed a large temporary earthwork near the besieged castle as a base for their assault. These siege castles were given nicknames, such as 'Bad Neighbour'. The construction of siege castles required teams of building workers, in addition to the military forces. Nearly eighty workmen were killed when such an earthwork collapsed in 1144.

The most dramatic fighting of the civil war took place in 1141. In February Stephen was besieging Lincoln Castle. Reinforcements for the garrison, led by Robert of Gloucester, arrived and a battle ensued. Stephen was captured

LEFT *Stephen's forces at Lincoln in 1141. Stephen was captured during the siege*

and taken as a prisoner to Bristol Castle. His future looked bleak, but Matilda squandered her advantage. In a battle outside the bishop's castle at Winchester her forces were defeated and she was forced to flee for her life while Robert of Gloucester was captured. Matilda, who, according to a contemporary monastic chronicler, 'was always superior to feminine softness and had a mind steeled and unbroken in adversity', fled to Devizes Castle. The urgency of the situation forced her to abandon her ladylike side-saddle and ride astride her horse like a man. An exchange of prisoners was arranged and Stephen was freed from Bristol in return for Robert.

A few months after the battle at Winchester Stephen once again came close to capturing Matilda, and she, once again, displayed her bravery and resolution. The king besieged Oxford Castle, where she was staying, for three months. It was Christmas-time and the garrison had almost run out of food. The king had placed numerous guards to ensure that no-one escaped, while his siege engines battered the walls of the castle. The countryside was covered in snow and ice and the River Thames had frozen over. Dressed in white for camouflage, Matilda and three knights successfully broke out of the castle by night on foot. Crossing the ice-covered river she made her way to the safety of nearby Wallingford. Even hostile chroniclers were impressed by Matilda's escape:

ABOVE *Miners try to destroy a castle wall, under the protection of a mobile shelter. The attackers drop 'Greek fire', a burning substance, on to their heads*

> In wondrous fashion she escaped unharmed through many enemies, through so many watchers in the silence of the night, whom the king had heedfully posted on every side of the castle. She left the castle by night, with three knights to accompany her, and went about six miles on foot, through the snow and the ice (for all the ground was white with an extremely heavy fall of snow and there was a very thick crust of ice on the water). What was the evident sign of a miracle, she crossed the waters dry-footed, without wetting her clothes at all. And by very great effort she reached the town of Wallingford during the night. (*Gesta Stephani*)

After the events at Lincoln, Winchester and Oxford the two sides reached a stalemate, which lasted for

several years. In 1147 Robert of Gloucester died and the following year Matilda retired to Normandy. Her son Henry attempted to renew the struggle in 1147 and 1149 without much success. In 1153 he invaded England once again with a larger force. With the Church providing mediation, Henry and Stephen agreed a peace treaty at Winchester by which Henry would inherit the throne in the event of Stephen's death. In October 1154 Stephen died and Henry II duly became king.

During these troubled years, as two sides struggled for the crown, local magnates used their castles to dominate, and sometimes to terrorise, their local areas. The writer of the *Anglo-Saxon Chronicle* graphically described the misery inflicted during the castle warfare of Stephen's reign:

> For every great man built him castles and held them against the king; and they filled the whole land with these castles. They sorely burdened the unhappy people of the country with forced labour on the castles; and when the castles were built, they filled them with devils and wicked men. By night and by day, they seized those whom they believed to have any wealth, whether they were men or women; and in order to get their gold and silver, they put them into prison and tortured them with unspeakable tortures.

Although the tortures were 'unspeakable', the chronicler went on to itemise them. The treatment of the prisoners included:
- hanging by the feet or by the thumbs;
- placing people in narrow chests, full of sharp stones;
- putting adders and other foul creatures in the dungeons.

The chronicler claimed that some of the instruments of torture were so heavy that it took two or three men to move them into position.

The peace treaty of 1153 stipulated that all the castles erected since the death of Henry I be destroyed. Once in power Henry vigorously enforced his authority by ordering the destruction of unauthorised baronial castles or by taking them into his own hands. In 1154 it has been calculated that there were about 224 significant baronial castles in active use and 49 royal castles. By 1214 the balance of power had altered and there were 179 baronial castles and 92 royal castles.

ABOVE *King Stephen's reign became known as 'the anarchy'. The nobility seized power in their local area, using castles as their bases*

ABOVE *Prisoners being tortured, from a drawing by the chronicler Matthew Paris. Paris describes how prisoners languishing in castles were regularly mistreated during the warfare of Stephen's reign*

THE KING AGAINST THE BARONS

ABOVE *Rochester Castle was seized by the baronial enemies of King John, then besieged by the irate king*

Another period of severe unrest, in which castles played a major role, occurred in the last days of the reign of King John (1199–1216). A number of leading barons clashed bitterly with the king over his financial exactions, and his fondness for giving important posts to humble foreigners rather than to members of their own class. At local level royal castles were a focus for this sense of grievance. In 1215 the barons went to war against the Crown and forced a number of concessions from King John when he agreed to the document known as Magna Carta. Significantly, several clauses of Magna Carta sought to curb the abuse of power by officials based in royal castles:

> No constable shall take anyone's corn or other chattels unless he pays on the spot in cash. No constable shall compel any knight to give money instead of castle-guard if he is willing to do the guard himself or through another good man. No sheriff, or bailiff of ours, shall take the horses or carts of any free man for transport work, save with the agreement of the free man. Neither we, nor our bailiffs, will take, for castles or other works of ours, timber which is not ours, except with the agreement of him whose timber it is.   (*Magna Carta, 1215*)

BELOW *An artist's impression of King John leading his troops during the siege of Rochester*

Magna Carta, although of great long-term significance, did not bring peace to England. The king reneged on his commitments and armed conflict again broke out between John and some of his barons. The centre of baronial power was in London. In September 1215, when John was staying at Dover Castle, the barons seized nearby Rochester Castle, apparently in order to block the road to London. John was enraged, and laid siege to Rochester. It was to become one of the most expensive and bitterly fought sieges in the history of medieval Britain, lasting two months. News of the siege clearly gripped the imagination of the monastic chroniclers of the time and they described the struggle in graphic terms:

> The siege was prolonged many days, owing to the great bravery and boldness of the besieged, who hurled stone for stone from the walls and ramparts on to the enemy. At last, after great numbers of the royal troops had been slain, the king, seeing that his warlike engines took but little effect, at length employed miners, who soon threw down a great part of the walls. The provisions of the besieged also failed them, and they were obliged to eat horses, and even their costly chargers. The soldiers of the king now rushed to the breaches in the walls, and by constant fierce assaults they forced the besieged to abandon the [outer part of the] castle, although not without great loss on their own side. The besieged then entered the tower. The king applied his miners to the tower, and an opening was made for the attackers.   (*Roger of Wendover*)

This account is supported by surviving government records. On 14 October John sent an urgent message to Canterbury ordering the manufacture 'by day and by night of as many picks as you are able'. These were clearly needed to undermine the walls. More surprisingly, on 25 November the king, who conducted the siege in person, ordered the despatch to Rochester 'with all speed by day and by night of forty of the fattest pigs of the sort least good for eating to bring fire beneath the tower'. By this stage the miners had

ABOVE *John antagonised many of his great nobles. This manuscript illustration shows one of his enemies offering him poisoned wine*

BELOW *A nineteenth-century painting showing the signing of Magna Carta in 1215. This document banned a number of abuses routinely practised by royal officials based in castles*

reached the keep and needed pig fat to help the fire they intended to start at the south-east corner of the keep.

The defenders at Rochester were extremely reluctant to surrender: they hoped that reinforcements might reach them from London. Their determination made them ruthless. weaker members of the garrison were driven out to conserve supplies for the remainder. John is said to have mutilated those who emerged by cutting off their hands and feet. Despite their efforts, the remaining defenders were eventually forced to give in. John's immediate inclination was to execute the entire garrison, but one of his men argued that this could be counter-productive as the baronial side might begin tit-for-tat killing:

And in his anger he ordered all the nobles to be hung on the gibbet. But Savaric de Mauleon standing before the king, said to him, My lord king, our war is not yet over, therefore you ought carefully to consider how the fortunes of war may change. If you hang these men, the barons, our enemies, will perhaps by a like event take me or other nobles of your army, and following your example, hang us.' The king, although unwillingly, listened to this advice and sent the noble prisoners to Corfe, Nottingham and other castles. All the soldiers, except the crossbow-men, he gave up to his own soldiers to be ransomed. Some of the crossbow-men who had slain many of his knights and soldiers during the siege, he ordered to be hung. *(Roger of Wendover)*

The advice that John was given was shrewd. Victory at Rochester did not bring an end to his conflict with the barons and he was still at war in 1216 when he died at Newark Castle.

47

LAW AND ORDER

While castles could be used against the Crown by a rebellious nobility, for much of the time the network of royal castles throughout England and Wales was a symbol of order and social stability. Royal castles often functioned as county gaols, and the hall of the castle was the place where the county court was held. This link between royal castles and law and order continues today. Some modern prisons, such as those at Oxford and Lancaster, are still housed within medieval castles.

Those accused of serious offences were kept in castles while they awaited trial. This cannot have been a pleasant experience. Castle gaolers were badly paid and so supplemented their income by charging prisoners for food and clothes and for the privilege of wearing lighter chains. By the time of sentencing most felons had no chattels left; presumably they had lost their property paying for their keep.

Few prisoners were convicts serving a prison sentence. If one were found guilty of almost any serious crime, including theft of any goods worth 12 pence or more, the punishment was hanging. Children could be hanged when they reached the age of twelve.

In the eleventh and twelfth centuries trials were sometimes conducted by 'ordeal', if the evidence of witnesses was inconclusive. The accused were forced to prove their innocence by withstanding ordeals such as holding a red hot iron or being plunged underwater. It was thought that if they were innocent God would intervene to protect them. Alongside this the more rational system of trial by jury was used. Trial by ordeal was condemned by the Church in 1215 and fell into abeyance.

The jury system in the Middle Ages was different from modern trial by jury. The juries were recruited from the 'hundred', or local area, in which the crime had been committed. Juries were expected to decide on the guilt or innocence of the accused based on their knowledge of the case. In modern terms they were both witnesses and jury. Juries appear to have been remarkably reluctant to convict. A study of criminal cases in eight counties between 1300 and 1348 shows an overall conviction rate of 22.9 per cent. Undoubtedly the fact that the only available punishment was hanging led many jurors to be lenient. Most jurors knew the families of the accused and were presumably unwilling to antagonise them. It is possible also that many regarded the months spent in gaol awaiting trial as sufficient punishment.

Sometimes the accused refused to plead. This was not an attractive option as it invariably led to death by torture. However, it had the advantage of preventing the Crown from seizing the chattels of the accused. The torture of those refusing to plead was known as 'peine forte et dure'. The process is described by the biographer of Edward II:

> When the suspect was brought before the justices, questioned and accused of many crimes, he did not answer. He was therefore thrust back into prison. The customary punishment for those mute of malice is carried out thus throughout the realm. The prisoner shall sit on the cold bare floor, dressed only in the thinnest of shirts, and pressed with as great a weight of iron as his wretched body can bear. His food shall be a little rotten bread, and his drink cloudy and stinking water. The day on which he eats he shall not drink, and the day on which he has drunk he shall not taste bread. Only superhuman strength survives this punishment beyond the fifth or sixth day. *(The Life of Edward II)*

Some prisoners became 'approvers'; that is, they confessed and agreed to name their accomplices and other guilty people. This was a desperate measure, usually chosen only when the prisoner was certain to be convicted, because many approvers were eventually hanged. The advantage of being an approver was that the prisoner's life was prolonged while arrangements were set in hand to arrest and try the named accomplices. Approvers were maintained at royal expense in prison, during which time they hoped to escape

ABOVE *Prisoners appearing before the king's justices. Prisoners were kept in royal castles until the arrival of the travelling justices*

ABOVE *A trial by combat illustrated in 1249. The use of ordeal and combat were gradually replaced by more rational means of deciding guilt*

BELOW *The Assize Court at York was built in the eighteenth century on the site of the medieval castle bailey. The link between royal castles and the administration of law and order often continued long after the castle had fallen out of residential and military use*

or win a royal pardon. Occasionally they were allowed to leave the country after the successful prosecution of their accomplices. If the named accomplices were acquitted, however, the approver was hanged. Approvers often claimed in court that they had been tortured by the gaoler and his staff and forced to make false accusations.

The administration of justice could be very inefficient. In the early fourteenth century William Leake was accused of stealing a horse at Boston in Lincolnshire. Although eventually judged innocent, William was held prisoner in Norwich Castle for two years until a jury from Lincolnshire was able to travel to Norwich to confirm his story. From around the same time we know of another prisoner at Norwich called Richard Sapling who spent at least seven years incarcerated waiting for the Chancery in London to confirm that his certificate of pardon, which had been damaged by water, was valid. On the day of a trial, proceedings were much brisker. At Norwich Castle an average of forty-six people was tried each day. Even if one assumes that the justices worked an arduous twelve-hour day, this works out at about fifteen minutes for each case. On one day in March 1316 the justices at Norwich dealt with seventy-one cases.

Female suspects made up about ten per cent of the total in the fourteenth century. This is quite close to the ratio still found in western Europe today. The courts were capable of com-

passion towards women prisoners. A woman named Agnes was held at Nottingham Castle from 1305 to 1306, accused of killing her daughter Rose, aged a year and a half. Agnes was from the Derbyshire village of Hathersage and was eventually taken for trial to Derby. The court was told how, at the time of the killing, Agnes had just given birth to another child and was lying in bed, with Rose in a nearby cradle. She was starving and fell into a delirium in which she imagined that a red dog had entered the house and was trying to eat little Rose. Agnes took a knife and, intending to kill the red dog, stabbed her child to death. The court accepted that she was out of her mind at the time of the killing and Agnes was pardoned.

Pregnant women could not be hanged because the Church insisted that the unborn child must be protected. Once they had given birth, the hanging could be carried out. We know of at least one woman who was able to extend her life by being almost constantly pregnant. Matilda Hereward of Northamptonshire was sentenced, with her husband, to hang in June 1301. On account of her pregnancy she was returned to gaol. However, visiting justices found her pregnant on each of their subsequent visits: in September 1301, January 1302, June 1302, October 1302, January 1303. After this date the records cease and we do not know how long Matilda was able to avoid the hangman.

ABOVE *A fifteenth-century illustration of prisoners being taken to execution. In reality, most accused prisoners were acquitted*

LEFT *The hall of a royal castle was also used as a courtroom. This artist's impression is of a trial in progress at Pickering Castle, Yorkshire*

OLD SARUM GAOL

ABOVE *The gatehouse at Old Sarum as it might have appeared in about 1130. Prisoners were brought here from across the county of Wiltshire*

Government records provide a full picture of the prisoners kept at Old Sarum Castle gaol in Wiltshire during the thirteenth and early fourteenth centuries. The gaol was a busy place, although it was emptied periodically when visiting justices came to Salisbury and the prisoners, for the most part, were freed or hanged. In January 1304, for example, it held over forty prisoners. About half of these were accused of murder, and the remainder of robbery, burglary and other crimes against property. In this sheep-rearing area many of the thefts were connected with the wool trade. The castle gaol does not appear to have been at all secure and escapes were common.

Throughout the country this was a time of some lawlessness, a situation that is reflected in the Old Sarum records. Criminal gangs roamed the region, and some of their members were highly mobile. John Martin, for example, who was hanged at Salisbury in 1275, had been born far away in Newcastle-upon-Tyne. His crime was to be one of a gang of robbers who operated at Glastonbury Fair. Violent gang members became known as 'trailbastons' because they carried, or trailed, large clubs called 'bastons'. Some were displaced former soldiers. In 1294 a large gang of twenty former soldiers, who had served together in

Gascony and deserted, was in the gaol at Old Sarum. They were held on suspicion because they had in their possession a large amount of money and valuable cloth. Their situation was evidently hopeless because, unusually, they pleaded guilty. Gang members often agreed to become approvers and to inform on their former colleagues. All the approvers in the Old Sarum records were ultimately hanged.

There are interesting examples from Old Sarum Castle of the principle of sanctuary. Criminals who successfully sought sanctuary in a church were allowed to 'abjure the realm'. This meant that, after they had stayed continuously in the church for forty nights and the county coroner had received their confession, they were obliged to take an oath promising to

ABOVE *Leg irons with chains and locks found at Castle Rising Castle, Norfolk*

BELOW *An outbreak of violence. Violent gangs known as trailbastons roamed the countryside*

leave the country. They were given a particular port of departure and a time limit by which they must have left the country. Exceeding this time limit or leaving the highway to the port was punishable by hanging. In fact there was considerable scope for disappearing between the church of sanctuary and the designated port. In 1277 a thief, caught red-handed and almost certain to be hanged, was being taken to the gaol at Old Sarum. On his way he made a dash into a neighbouring church. His guards broke the rules of sanctuary by entering the church and removing him. The royal justices took exception to the guards' action and they paid a high price for their transgression:

> Richard Hutte, taken with stolen wool by the men of Melksham, escaped from their custody to St Peter's church whence he was removed. It is adjudged that he be restored to the church and the men of the manor be fined 100s for the escape. And he is restored to the church.

The ultimate fate of Richard Hutte is unknown. Some of those who found sanctuary could not bring themselves to leave the country and risked execution. In 1302 the Old Sarum gaol held one John le Bakere. He had previously sought sanctuary and had been allowed to abjure the realm. However, he failed to reach his assigned port and was re-arrested.

> John le Bakere was assigned Portsmouth as his port, had one and a half days for his passage, and has now returned without warrant. He confesses that he has not kept his days' journeys. So hanged.

If a crime was committed jointly by a husband and wife, the wife could escape conviction on the grounds that she was subject to her husband and obliged to obey his criminal orders. An example of this can be found in the Old Sarum records. In 1276 Edith de Helmerton was held in the castle gaol. She and her husband Robert had been taken stealing sheep at Alton Priors, and Robert was hanged. Edith was pregnant and was kept in gaol until the birth of her baby. A jury was then convened and asked to decide whether or not she was lawfully married to Robert. The jury declared that she was Robert's 'espoused wife' and so she was released.

Surprisingly, members of the clergy often took part in crime in medieval times. They had the advantage of being exempt from capital punishment. Criminals who could prove that they were clergymen were handed over to the diocesan authorities for punishment, which often consisted of imprisonment in the bishop's gaol. In 1289 we find Nicholas de Kyngeston, accused of several larcenies, claiming 'benefit of clergy'. The gaoler, Adam, tried to assist him, presumably in return for a bribe, by shaving his head so that he looked like a tonsured priest. This was discovered by the justices who ordered the arrest of the gaoler. We do not know what became of Nicholas.

The Wiltshire juries sometimes took a lenient view of local criminals. In 1306 John Burgeys was accused of breaking and entering. It was claimed that he had stolen goods worth 40 pence. John was obviously guilty of the burglary, for which the obligatory penalty was death. However, the jury managed to help him avoid the noose by declaring that the goods concerned were worth less than 12 pence:

> The jurors say that he was needy and in want and entered the house and took goods to the value of eight pence, namely bread and cheese and other small things. Quit for the smallness of his theft. Six weeks' prison.

CASTLES AND THEIR SHERIFFS

Local administration did not always operate smoothly or fairly. The king's representative in each county was the sheriff, or 'shire-reeve', a post that had developed in Anglo-Saxon times and was retained after the Norman Conquest. Often in county towns the sheriff was also constable of the castle, which he used as his headquarters. Sheriffs were responsible for:

✤ organisation of royal justice;
✤ collection of taxes;
✤ management of the royal estates.

The responsibility for taxation and other forms of revenue-raising often made sheriffs unpopular. They were given financial targets by the Exchequer in London, and this money was known as the 'farm of the county'. The agreed sum was handed over every year at Michaelmas and was recorded on 'pipe rolls' – a number of sheepskin membranes, fastened together and rolled up. The earliest surviving pipe roll dates from the reign of Henry I.

This shows for example that at Michaelmas 1130, Miles, the sheriff of Gloucestershire, paid £222 13s for the 'farm of the county'. It also lists his expenses, which included over £7 spent on building work at Gloucester Castle, and payments to the staff at St Briavel's Castle 'for a knight and serjeants and a door-keeper and a watchman'.

The system of revenue-raising gave sheriffs considerable scope for corruption and extortion. Throughout the Middle Ages there were complaints about the exactions of the sheriffs. In 1170 Henry II ordered an Inquest of Sheriffs – a nationwide commission into the impositions of the sheriffs:

At this time the king removed from office almost all the sheriffs of England and their bailiffs because they had evil treated the men of his realm. Afterwards the king caused all the men of the realm to give true testimony concerning the things of which the sheriffs and their men had deprived them. But the people of England suffered considerable loss in this matter, since after the inquisition had taken place the king restored some of the sheriffs to office, and they afterwards imposed even greater impositions than before.
(*The deeds of King Henry II*)

About a century later a political song criticised the sheriffs for their corruption. The song also refers to the power the sheriff had to force people to sit on juries against their will.

Who can truly tell
How cruel sheriffs are?
Of their hardness to poor people
No tale can go too far.
If a man cannot pay
They drag him here and there.
They put him on assizes,
The juror's oath to swear.
He dares not breathe a murmur,
Or he has to pay again,
And the saltiness of the sea
Is less bitter than his pain.

Great nobles often resented the power of the local sheriff, which threatened to rival their own. This resentment was heightened by the fact that sheriffs often came from relatively humble sections of the nobility. Kings were often keen to appoint men from a poorer background on the grounds that they would be more loyal. This trend was particularly marked during the reign of King John, who appointed a number of obscure foreigners as sheriffs, to the intense annoyance of the great nobility. Pressure from these nobles ensured that the first version of Magna Carta required the dismissal of specific unpopular sheriffs.

The most famous of the adventurer-sheriffs was Falkes de Bréauté, the illegitimate son of a knight in Normandy. Falkes was not a gentle man. According to contemporary chroniclers his strange first name came from the Latin word 'falx', meaning 'the scythe'.

ABOVE *An armed man terrorises the poor. He wears the livery of the great nobleman William Marshal*

ABOVE *The medieval countryside was often violent, and sheriffs provided rough justice. This eleventh-century drawing shows a tough-looking band of armed peasants*

LEFT *Henry II's effigy at Fontevraud Abbey in France. Powerful kings such as Henry used royal castles – and their sheriffs – to control the local community*

As a boy in Normandy he had killed a knight with a scythe in his father's meadow. Falkes made his reputation during the reign of King John as a tough military governor of Glamorgan.

John could be generous to his supporters and he rewarded Falkes handsomely. In 1216 Falkes controlled the counties and royal castles of Northamptonshire, Oxfordshire, Bedfordshire-Buckinghamshire and Cambridge-Huntingdonshire. King John also forced a rich noble widow to marry him. Men such as Falkes used their power to exploit and terrorise people living near his castles and to browbeat any opponents. In January 1217 Falkes attacked the abbey at St Albans as night fell. His army was made up of men from his various castles. He forced the abbot to hand over £100 before agreeing to leave.

Not surprisingly, Falkes's activities won him many enemies. The most determined of these was the Earl of Pembroke, who called him 'this capricious and evil man'. Pembroke had previously clashed with Falkes over the control of land in the counties over which Falkes was the sheriff. Unfortunately for Falkes, his enemies eventually got the upper hand after the death of his patron, King John. In 1224 the government began to take back the royal castles controlled by Falkes. He responded by strengthening the garrison at Bedford, one of his remaining strongholds. Falkes's ally, his brother William, kidnapped a royal judge and took him as a prisoner to

Bedford Castle. Although Falkes himself was not inside the castle, a government army was sent to Bedford and an eight-week siege followed. William and the garrison refused to give in and the castle was taken by force. Unusually, the whole of the garrison of over eighty men was then executed. Falkes was now powerless and he surrendered to the king. His life was spared but he lost all his lands and was forced into exile. He died in Italy in 1226, supposedly from eating bad fish. The monks of St Albans never forgave him, including Matthew Paris who described his death with evident satisfaction:

> He died poisoned, having surfeited himself with poison fish. After taking his supper he lay down to sleep, and was discovered dead, black, stinking and rotten. Thus reaping the fruits of his works, he miserably closed his sinful life.
> (*Matthew Paris*)

falco de Brea

CASTLE TOWNS

ABOVE *A walled town in the fourteenth century, from the Luttrell Psalter*

ABOVE *Neighbouring towns were often looted during the siege of castles*

ABOVE *This aerial photograph of Richmond in Yorkshire shows how the castle dominated the medieval town centre*

Towns and castles were closely associated from the time of the Conquest. The Normans realised that towns were potential centres of resistance against their rule and used castles to neutralise this threat. Having won the Battle of Hastings William the Conqueror's next move was to ensure control of London. Even after his coronation there William felt vulnerable and he moved to Barking 'while certain strongholds were made in the town against the fickleness of the vast and fierce populace.' Almost certainly one of these early strongholds was the Tower of London, strategically placed to control the passage of ships into the city. It was several years before Norman control of the country was completely secure, and the process of subduing the English went hand-in-hand with the construction of castles in the major centres of population. In 1068 the citizens of Exeter refused to acknowledge William as their king. William marched in person to the city and showed his ruthlessness by blinding a hostage in front of the city walls. Exeter soon capitulated and William immediately 'selected a spot within the walls for the erection of a castle'. Later in the same year he established castles and garrisons in Warwick, Nottingham, York, Lincoln, Huntingdon and Cambridge. Overall, twenty royal castles were built in major towns between 1066 and 1100, and a number of trusted barons also established castles in key towns.

At first the castle was a symbol of the military power through which the Normans held their newly conquered land. The nature of the relationship between the government and the townsfolk was illustrated by the way hundreds of houses were sometimes demolished to make way for the new castle. Ordinary townsfolk had no redress against arbitrary action of this kind. The Church was a little more successful in seeking compensation. In 1069 leading churchmen condemned the way in which government forces had taken part of the abbey cemetery at Worcester when building the castle. Over 150 years later the monks of Worcester were still complaining about this affront to their rights. When King John died in 1216 and was buried at Worcester the monks reminded the government of the way the castle encroached upon their land. The government gave way and handed over control of the castle bailey to the abbey.

Once the Conquest was an established fact, and ideas of rebellion a distant memory, castles in towns continued to function as centres for government and the administration of justice. Later in the Middle Ages many town castles lost their military significance but remained locally important as the place where the county court was held.

A significant Jewish community established itself in England after the Conquest, and enjoyed royal protection. The Jews offered valuable financial services to kings and noblemen and were a source of taxation revenue to the government. As the only non-Christians in the country, however, they were a vulnerable minority and they looked to the royal castle for protection. The 'Jewry' (Jewish district) was often close to the castle. There was a virulent strain of anti-Jewish prejudice in twelfth-century England. This reached its worst point in March 1190 when the Jews of York were attacked by local people. They took refuge in York Castle and, not trusting the constable, refused him re-entry after he had left the castle on business. The constable and the sheriff of Yorkshire then besieged the castle. Seeing that their situation was hopeless, on the night of 16 March the majority of the Jewish community committed suicide within the castle. The few survivors gave themselves up and were put to death by their Christian neighbours.

When castles in towns were involved in military conflict the victims were often the local people. Lincoln Castle was the scene of fighting on two occasions. In both instances few of the contending knights were killed but large numbers of townsfolk were slain. In 1141 Lincoln was the scene of a battle between King Stephen and the forces of the Empress Matilda (see page 44). Stephen was captured and treated with great courtesy, but the victors' chivalry did not extend to the townsfolk of Lincoln, many of whom were put to death. This fact is recounted merely in passing, and with approval, by the contemporary historian William of Malmesbury:

> Therefore the glorious Earl of Gloucester gave orders that the king should be kept alive and unharmed, not suffering even that he should be the victim of any insulting language. But the mass of the burgesses of Lincoln was in great part cut down through the just anger of the victors.

Several decades later the ordinary people of Lincoln were again the innocent victims of warfare. In 1217 the armies of the French prince Louis, and the royalists loyal to the boy-king Henry III, met at Lincoln. Remarkably, although fighting took place through the streets of the town, hardly any of the noble combatants were killed. The local people fared less well, however:

> Many of the women of the city were drowned in the river. To avoid trouble they had taken to small boats, with their children, female servants, and household property, and perished on their journey. The boats were over-loaded, and the women not knowing how to manage the boats, all perished, for business done in haste is always badly done.   (Roger of Wendover)

Towns were, on occasion, scenes of tumult and riot and the local castle, as a symbol of authority, was sometimes a target during disturbances. In 1381, during the Peasants' Revolt, the rebels ransacked the Tower of London and beheaded the Archbishop of Canterbury who was taking refuge there. A less famous episode occurred at Bristol in 1313. The people of Bristol rose up in revolt against the small group of wealthy citizens who controlled the government of the city. Violence broke out and the sheriff tried to restore law and order. The people turned on the sheriff and he was forced to take refuge in his castle. The people besieged the castle and wrecked some of the castle property that lay outside the fortifications. The moat was drained and the castle mill destroyed.

> They forcibly impeded the constable and beat, wounded and imprisoned his deputies. In divers places in the town they made barricades, not permitting victuals to be carried to the castle. They made frequent attacks on the men who were in the castle, by shooting arrows and quarrels into the castle, and finally they erected and crenellated a wall of stone and lime in Wynche Street and made barricades opposite the castle, discharging arrows and quarrels through the battlements. (Government records, 1313)

ABOVE *An artist's impression of the fire at York Castle as the Jewish community inside committed mass suicide*

ABOVE *In 1381 the Arch-bishop of Canterbury was killed as a mob rampaged through the Tower of London*

BELOW *The siege of Lincoln, 1217. The people of the town were the innocent victims of this conflict*

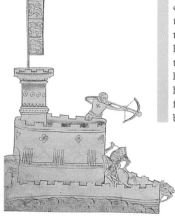

THE DECLINE OF THE CASTLE

By the late Middle Ages castles had lost much of their military importance. They became 'show castles', where kings and great lords carried out chivalric ritual. Many powerful nobles and monarchs now chose to build unfortified houses instead of less comfortable castles. Most castles became ruined and neglected until people began to take an interest in the heritage of the Middle Ages.

THE LONG TWILIGHT OF THE CASTLE

ABOVE *Edward III in the robes of the Order of the Garter, which he founded as an expression of his chivalric ideals*

For many castles the process of neglect and decline began early in the Middle Ages. Hundreds of motte-and-bailey castles lost their military significance at an early stage and fell into disuse. By the end of the twelfth century in England the earth and timber castles that had predominated during the first century of Norman rule had become obsolete in military terms. Those structures that were not converted into stone fell into decay. The adoption of stone as the preferred building material inevitably limited the ownership of functioning castles to a smaller group of wealthy nobles who could afford to build and maintain them.

While fewer nobles could afford to build castles in the later Middle Ages, the nature of the castle was also changing. In the early Middle Ages castles were, above all, a practical response to the social and military circumstances of the time. In the later Middle Ages castle design was influenced less by practical considerations and more by a sense of

what would impress onlookers. The designers of many castles built after the reign of Edward I seem to have been less concerned with warfare and more anxious to provide a theatrical setting for a grand lifestyle. Historians have called these buildings 'show castles' or 'castles of chivalry'.

The tendency towards the 'castle of chivalry' is most clearly evident in Edward III's redevelopment of Windsor Castle. A prolific builder, Edward invested his greatest efforts in this scheme, which was intended to provide a fitting backdrop for his chivalric lifestyle. Between 1350 and 1377 over £50,000 was spent on the castle. Little of the money was used to strengthen the military potential of the castle, but was spent instead on making the accommodation and the chapel more splendid. Significantly, in the rebuilding of Windsor, Edward was advised not by a great soldier but by a clergyman, William of Wykeham, who later founded Winchester College and New College, Oxford:

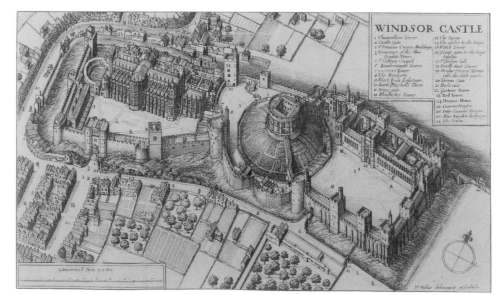

WINDSOR CASTLE

LEFT *Edward's redevelopment of Windsor was concerned with display and did little to improve the military significance of the castle*

ABOVE *The Windsor of the late Middle Ages was intended as a latterday Camelot. This fifteenth-century illustration shows King Arthur presiding over a tournament*

ABOVE *Kirby Muxloe Castle in Leicestershire dates from the late fifteenth century. Built in brick, the castle was designed to impress onlookers*

About the year of our Lord 1359 our lord the king, at the instance of William Wikham, clerk, caused many excellent buildings in the castle of Windsor to be thrown down, and others more beautiful and sumptuous to be set up. The said William was of very low birth yet he was very shrewd, and a man of great energy. Considering how he could please the king and secure his goodwill, he counselled him to build the said castle of Windsor in the form in which it appears today to the beholder.   (*Polychronicon*)

Edward loved tournaments and the world of chivalry and he was captivated by tales of Arthurian legend. He founded a new order of chivalry in 1348 and regarded Windsor as a latter-day Camelot. Windsor was the stage on which his chivalric fantasies were played out and no expense or luxury was spared. Between 1350 and 1354, for example, Italian craftsmen installed a great clock in the keep at Windsor. This is the earliest known mechanical clock in England.

Although some of the great nobility built new castles in the fourteenth and fifteenth centuries, these were also, for the most part, 'show castles'. They had military features but were primarily designed to impress onlookers. Examples include Caister (Norfolk), Hurstmonceux and Kirby Muxloe (Leicestershire), and Tattershall (Lincolnshire). At all these castles the builders made use of brick, a material which became fashionable in an age that enjoyed the bright and the gaudy.

In the fourteenth and fifteenth centuries castles continued to be the home of large noble households. Such households were themselves undergoing important changes. They no longer moved once or even twice a month but became much more static, and by 1380 most households were staying in one place for several months at a time. This decreased mobility coincided with a steep rise in the size of households. Studies of household accounts suggest that while in 1300 a typical noble household employed about fifty people, by 1400 the number had doubled. On the other hand, the traditional bonds of feudal loyalty became less important. Instead, the relationship between a great lord and his retainers was cemented by cash. Those lords with sufficient money entered into contracts or 'indentures' with members of their household, offering cash and clothes in return for loyalty. Historians call this 'bastard feudalism'. Members of the household wore a livery – a distinctive set of clothes to identify the lord to whom they owed their loyalty. Senior members of the household appear to have had rising expectations about their accommodation. In many castles the buildings were substantially altered between 1350 and 1500 to provide more comfortable chambers for senior officers. In some cases these powerful retainers won a reputation for violence and many people were alarmed by their lawless behaviour. Successive kings condemned the excesses of the household retainers and tried to curb their behaviour:

Grievous complaint and clamour hath been made unto us of great and outrageous oppressions in divers parts of the realm. Many are encouraged and made bold in their evil deeds because they be of the retinue of lords, with fees, robes and liveries of company. We have ordained that no man give any manner of such livery to knight or esquire if he is not retained with him for the term of his life, in peace and war, by indenture. (*Richard II, 1390*)

The king wills that no lord shall knowingly receive, keep in household or maintain thieves, robbers, oppressors of the people, those guilty of manslaughter, ravishers of women, and other open and notorious perpetrators of misdeeds, upon penalty of the king's great displeasure and the perils that may ensue therefrom. (*Edward IV, 1461*)

ABOVE *A wild boar badge, worn by members of the household of Richard III*

ABOVE *Henry VII returns from a tournament surrounded by uniformed members of his household*

THE BEGINNING OF THE END

ABOVE *The 'Boxted Bombard', a large cannon from about 1450. There is no evidence that the advent of gunpowder caused the decline of the castle in late medieval Britain*

BELOW *Clifford's Tower, York in 1730. Castles such as this lost their military significance in the late Middle Ages. Later still some castle remains came to be used as romantic follies: here the keep and mound have been incorporated into the garden of a prosperous eighteenth-century gentleman, whose comfortable new house can be seen to the bottom right*

The last royal castle to be built in England during the Middle Ages was Queenborough Castle on the Isle of Sheppey (demolished in the seventeenth century). The castle was begun by Edward III in 1361 and was intended to defend the Thames estuary against the possibility of a French invasion. Between 1370 and 1500 the kings of England built no new castles, although they did repair and maintain several existing ones. Many royal castles lost their military purpose and remained significant only for their judicial functions. Lincoln, for example, was a place of great strategic importance in the early Middle Ages, but from the fourteenth century the castle functioned simply as the site of the county gaol and the county court. Similarly, at Northampton the only buildings in the castle on which significant money was spent in the fourteenth and fifteenth centuries were the hall, where the county court was held, and the gaol. Other royal castles were more neglected still, as is indicated by this report on Shrewsbury Castle in 1443:

All the housing within our Castle of Salop is fallen down and nothing left but only the walls which, unless they be mended and covered, are likely within a short time to fall. The dungeon [keep] of our said castle is by the course of the River of Severn undermined and great parts thereof are fallen down into the said river.

Some people attribute the decline of the castle to the advent of gunpowder. In fact there is, in Britain, little evidence to support the theory that castles decayed because of the introduction of guns and heavy artillery. The use of gunpowder was invented in China, possibly in the ninth century AD, but the technology was slow to spread and the earliest European illustration of a gun dates from 1327. For a long time guns were used alongside stone-throwing machines. The first guns were not powerful enough to demolish strong walls and were used against easier targets, such as wooden gates and the buildings within a castle. It was not until the fifteenth century that technology had developed further and guns were able

ABOVE *Stokesay Castle, Shropshire was more of a fortified manor house than a castle. The great hall has large windows facing outwards, a security risk that would not have been tolerated in a castle intended to have serious defensive capabilities*

ABOVE *Raglan Castle has gunports so that the defenders could use guns, but in other respects the design pays little attention to the dangers of artillery bombardment*

to demolish most stone walls. There are many examples of gunports or gunloops – modified openings in castle walls for the use of small guns – from the late fourteenth century, but in other respects the advent of the gun made little difference to the design of castles in Britain. This contrasts with France, where by the fifteenth century the designers of fortifications began to create substantial bulwarks that could absorb much of the impact of a cannon ball. Raglan Castle in Gwent, substantially built in the 1460s by the Earl of Pembroke, is typical of the period. Although its walls do possess gun loops, the fundamental design takes little account of the dangers of artillery bombardment. This seems to be because by the late Middle Ages warfare in England and Wales only rarely took the form of major sieges and was much more likely to be settled by a pitched battle, fought in open countryside.

A decline in the strategic significance of the castle coincided with an increase in the construction of unfortified palaces and houses. Kings and great nobles had always possessed unfortified dwellings. In London, for example, the royal family could choose between a castle in the form of the Tower of London and the unfortified Palace of Westminster. The palaces and great houses of the late fourteenth and fifteenth centuries were typically built around two or more large courtyards. These courtyards were less constricted than castle wards and allowed for the provision of substantial private accommodation for senior members of the household. In the 1390s John Holand, later the Duke of Exeter,

decided to build himself a new property in Devon. He was extremely wealthy and well connected and perfectly capable of building himself a castle but instead he chose to build Dartington Hall. Dartington is one of the earliest surviving examples of the type of courtyard house that began to supplant the castle as the preferred residence of the powerful.

While the great nobility of Devon could afford to be relaxed about their personal security, the gentry of Ireland, Scotland and the most northerly English counties remained vulnerable to armed attack. As a result, between 1300 and 1600 rectangular tower houses were built throughout Ireland and Scotland. Similar houses were built in the far north of England and are generally known as 'pele towers'. Some of them are relatively humble: the pele tower in Corbridge, Northumberland, is no more than the local vicar's house built in the form of a tower. The tower houses of Scotland and Ireland were often much more elaborate than this. Some followed an L-shaped design to provide more living space. Famous castles, such as Glamis in Scotland and Blarney Castle in Ireland, began life as late medieval tower houses.

ABOVE *The south tower at Stokesay (top left of picture) gives an impression of strength not followed through elsewhere. The castle was built in a period of relative peace and prosperity*

THE CASTLE SINCE THE MIDDLE AGES

Unsettled conditions in Ireland, Scotland and the northernmost English counties meant that tower houses continued to be built well into the seventeenth century. In most of England and Wales, by contrast, from the beginning of the sixteenth century the idea of the fortified residence was an anachronism. The castle had always combined both defence and residence, and the great houses that were built during the reign of Henry VIII – such as Hampton Court and Nonsuch Palace in Surrey – were in no sense military structures. In 1511 the Duke of Buckingham began the construction of Thornbury Castle near Bristol. (The building was incomplete in 1522 when the duke was executed.) Although it was called a castle, Thornbury was not designed for serious warfare. Henry VIII did build new fortifications in the form of coastal forts, but they were not intended as royal homes.

Between 1535 and 1545 the antiquary John Leland visited several hundreds of castles and made detailed comments on 258 of them. Only about a third were in a sound condition. A large number were ruinous including many of the most substantial. The decline that Leland noticed in the first half of the sixteenth century gathered pace in the following decades. A document of 1561 relates, for example, that the bailey of Peak Castle in Derbyshire was only reprieved from demolition on the grounds that it was useful as a pound for stray animals. By 1575 one observer, William Harrison, was writing:

> It seemeth by our experience that we here in England suppose castles altogether unneedful. At this present there are very few or no castles maintained within England, saving only upon the coasts and marches of the country.

The English Civil War (1642–51) briefly transformed the status of the castle. After many years of peaceful neglect fortifications again became an important part of daily life. Many castles were in such a decayed state that they could make no useful contribution to the conflict. Both sides sought to construct earthworks outside castle and town walls in order to make them capable of resisting artillery. At Cambridge, for example, where the castle had been abandoned as a military structure since the fifteenth century, the military governor was able to report by 1643: 'Our town and castle are now very strongly fortified being encompassed with breastworks and bulwarks.' Many castles were damaged in the fighting; at Scarborough, for example, the west front of the keep was demolished by Parliamentary artillery. A far greater number of castles were damaged after the fighting was over as a result of a policy of deliberate demolition, known as 'slighting'. By slighting a castle commanders ensured that it would not be used again by the enemy as a stronghold. The scale of the slighting varied from place to place. A thorough job was done at Winchester, where only the hall of this great royal castle was left standing. In a more partial demolition at Helmsley in Yorkshire the curtain wall was reduced to near ground level and half the keep was pulled down. Fallen stonework from the keep still lies in the ditch. Demolishing sections of a large castle was no easy matter and the work often took several months. However, financial accounts show that slighting

 BELOW *Pendennis Castle, Cornwall. Although Henry VIII was keen to develop such coastal defences, he actually lived far away in the comfort of palaces such as Hampton Court and Nonsuch*

LEFT *An artist's impression of the gun deck at Pendennis in the 1540s*

ABOVE *The keep at Scarborough (Yorkshire) was extensively damaged by artillery fire during the Civil War*

could be a cost-effective exercise. The demolition work at Pontefract Castle in Yorkshire was carried out by sixteen men over a ten-week period at a cost of £777. The sale of materials realised £1540 for the lead and £201 for the timber.

The lure of the materials meant that some demolition continued after the Restoration of the Monarchy (1660). There was little sense that medieval castles were part of a shared heritage and deserved preservation. In 1660 a group of Caernarfon residents proposed that their local castle, arguably the finest in the whole of Britain, should be demolished. Some damage was done but the demolition plan was eventually shelved. In 1665 lead and timber were taken from Conwy Castle and it was left without a roof. The top of the magnificent early keep at Colchester Castle was demolished in 1683.

Attitudes towards the Middle Ages began to change in the eighteenth century and the idea of castles as 'romantic' places emerged. Gradually, educated people came to believe that the medieval heritage of great castles was something precious that ought to be cherished and preserved. At the beginning of the nineteenth century the antiquary Richard Colt Hoare expressed this growing sense of respect and admiration when he visited the castle at Conwy, which had nearly been demolished 150 years earlier:

> For a short interval the road becomes uninteresting – when Conway's proud towers burst suddenly upon the sight. The castle itself is a most noble structure and of the most picturesque form. The whole is so beautiful in all its parts and so judiciously situated that I could almost suppose the artist, not the engineer, had directed its construction.

A few great medieval castles have remained as family homes: these include the royal castle of Windsor and private castles at Arundel, Warwick and Berkeley. Whereas these castles have been continuously maintained by their owners, the majority of medieval castles were ruinous by the early nineteenth century. Paradoxically, the industrialisation and urbanisation of the nineteenth century contributed to a growing sense of respect for Britain's medieval heritage. A growing sense of responsibility for the physical remains of the past led to the passing of the Ancient Monuments Act in 1882. From this point the government accepted that it had a role to play in the conservation and care of historic monuments, including medieval castles – a tradition that is continued today by English Heritage and others.

RIGHT *A romantic view of Brougham Castle, Cumbria painted in about 1800*

61

WHAT REMAINS TO BE SEEN

❖ BARNARD CASTLE (*above*), Durham. Located on a high cliff next to the River Tees, the castle dominates the town which grew up around it. Its great round tower dates from the early thirteenth century.

BEAUMARIS, Anglesey. A classic concentric castle, with two large gatehouses and a dock linking it to the sea. The last great castle built for Edward I by Master James of St George, it was begun in 1295 and never finished.

❖ BEESTON, Cheshire. The castle is built in a spectacular cliff-top location. There are two substantial circuits of walls and a fine gatehouse dating from the 1220s.

❖ BELSAY, Northumberland. Built during a period of conflict between the English and Scots. A seventeenth-century house is attached to the late fourteenth-century tower.

❖ BERRY POMEROY, Devon. The medieval home of the Pomeroy family, the castle was substantially rebuilt in a Renaissance style by Edward Seymour, Duke of Somerset, in the sixteenth century. There is a fifteenth-century gatehouse.

BODIAM, East Sussex. An attractive, well-preserved late fourteenth-century four-sided castle, with strong corner towers and extensive water defences.

CAERNARFON, Gwynedd. The most ambitious of all the great castles built by Edward I, and the centre for the rule of north Wales after Edward's conquest. The castle has unusual polygonal wall towers with banded masonry reminiscent of Constantinople.

CAERPHILLY, Caerphilly. Arguably the finest of all the non-royal castles, it was begun in 1271 and belonged to the rich Clare family. The concentric castle with water defences is on an enormous scale.

❖ CARLISLE (*below left*), Cumbria. This substantial castle includes visible remains ranging from a twelfth-century great tower to modern military architecture.

CARREG CENNEN, Dyfed. Located spectacularly on a cliff-top high above the River Cennen, the present building dates largely from the thirteenth and fourteenth centuries.

❖ CASTLE ACRE, Norfolk. A fortified house of the eleventh century built by one of the Conqueror's close friends, William de Warenne, shortly after the Conquest. It was extended and strengthened in the early twelfth century.

❖ CASTLE RISING, Norfolk. The elaborate keep dates from about 1140. It features a well-preserved forebuilding and staircase.

CHEPSTOW, Monmouthshire. This great baronial border castle has an impressive setting on a cliff-top above the River Wye. The tower dates back to the late eleventh century while a substantial new hall and other buildings were added in the late thirteenth century.

COLCHESTER, Essex. Built by William the Conqueror, this was one of the first stone castles in England. The remains of the massive great tower can still be seen.

❖ CONISBROUGH, South Yorkshire. The remains comprise a magnificent cylindrical keep with projecting buttresses.

CONWY (*above*), Conwy. The riverside castle, built by Edward I, is organised around two courtyards and has eight massive towers. The associated town walls also survive.

CORFE, Dorset. A major castle before its partial demolition during the English Civil War, with a large keep dating from about 1100. It was the favourite castle of King John, who built the 'Gloriette', a courtyard residence.

❖ DOVER, Kent. One of the most significant royal castles in England. The twelfth-century keep is the largest in the country, while the magnificent Constable's Gate dates from the early thirteenth century.

❖ DUNSTANBURGH, Northumberland. This seaside castle, with its enormous enclosing wall, was begun in 1313 as a power base for the Earl of Lancaster.

❖ FRAMLINGHAM, Suffolk. Built in the late twelth century, this was one of the first castles to rely solely on a strong curtain wall and to do without a keep.

❖ GOODRICH (*above*), Herefordshire. The castle belonged to the great nobleman William Marshal in the early thirteenth century. The tower dates from the twelfth century, but there was substantial rebuilding, with massive new walls and towers, in about 1300; there are extensive remains of residential accommodation from this period.

HARLECH, Gwynedd. Built by Edward I between 1283 and 1289 in a dramatic cliff-top location, the castle has a majestic gatehouse and powerful curtain walls with huge drum towers at the wall angles.

❖ HELMSLEY, North Yorkshire. The defences include an impressive and unusual double ditch. The curtain wall, towers and keep of the inner ward date from about 1200.

❖ KENILWORTH, Warwickshire. The keep is twelfth-century, with water defences added in the thirteenth century. The castle was the scene of a prolonged siege in 1266. A great hall and accommodation were added in the late fourteenth century.

❖ KIRBY MUXLOE, Leicestershire. This rectangular moated castle, built in brick, was begun in 1480 but never finished due to the execution of its owner, William, Lord Hastings.

LAUNCESTON *(above)*, Cornwall. The motte is capped by a stone shell keep. In the thirteenth century a cylindrical tower was built within the shell keep.

LEEDS, Kent. This picturesque castle is set in massive water defences. It was bought by Edward I in 1298 and remained a royal castle for the rest of the Middle Ages. A favourite residence of several medieval kings.

LEWES, East Sussex. This highly unusual castle had two mottes. There is also a twelfth-century gatehouse.

THE TOWER OF LONDON. The riverside fortress is dominated by the White Tower, the great stone tower built by the Conqueror to provide palatial accommodation; it also contains the beautiful chapel of St John. The fortress is enclosed by late thirteenth-century curtain walls.

LUDLOW, Shropshire. Built without a motte or keep, the castle has early stone walls dating to about 1100 and a late thirteenth-century great hall.

LYDFORD, Devon. The tower, dating from 1195 but substantially rebuilt in the thirteenth century, was used as a prison throughout the Middle Ages. Nearby there are traces of Saxon town defences and an early Norman castle.

MIDDLEHAM, North Yorkshire. One of the favourite castles of Richard III, Middleham has a large keep built in about 1170 and a curtain wall and tower added in the thirteenth and fourteenth centuries.

NEWCASTLE-UPON-TYNE, Tyne & Wear. The building which gave its name to the city has a twelfth-century keep and a thirteenth-century gatehouse.

OKEHAMPTON, Devon. The twelfth-century keep was built on an earlier motte. There are also a fourteenth-century great hall and accommodation.

ORFORD, Suffolk. The distinctive polygonal keep was built by Henry II to an unusual design with three projecting buttress towers.

PEAK, Derbyshire. The castle is dramatically sited on the hills of the Peak District. The small keep dates from the reign of Henry II.

PORTCHESTER, Hampshire. Built in the corner of a surviving Roman coastal fort, the remains include a large twelfth-century keep and fourteenth-century lodgings.

PEMBROKE, Dyfed. There are substantial remains dating from about 1200, including a large cylindrical keep and gatehouse.

PEVENSEY, East Sussex. Built on the site of the first castle raised by William the Conqueror, the remains are dominated by substantial thirteenth-century walls and wall towers.

PICKERING, North Yorkshire. The large eleventh-century motte is crowned by a ruined early thirteenth-century shell-keep. Substantial portions of the curtain wall and towers survive.

RAGLAN, Monmouthshire. Raglan is unusual in being a relatively intact castle built entirely in the fifteenth century. There is a massive gatehouse and a very late example of a keep.

RESTORMEL, Cornwall. A late twelfth-century circular wall is encircled by an earlier ditch and large bank. In the late thirteenth century this was the residence of the Earl of Cornwall, who added accommodation inside the ring wall.

RHUDDLAN, Denbighshire. An early castle of Edward I, it has a concentric design and substantial inner wall.

RICHMOND *(above)*, North Yorkshire. This large castle is sited on a cliff above the River Swale. It has some very early (eleventh-century) stone buildings, including a hall and a twelfth-century keep. William the Lion, King of Scotland, was imprisoned here.

ROCHESTER, Kent. Sited immediately adjacent to the Norman cathedral, the castle's most impressive feature is the keep, begun in 1127. This was the scene of a protracted siege in 1216 (see pages 46–47).

OLD SARUM, Wiltshire. The Norman castle was built within massive Iron Age earthworks. A cathedral was also sited within the enclosure before it was moved to New Sarum or Salisbury.

SCARBOROUGH, North Yorkshire. The castle has a twelfth-century keep and is positioned dramatically on a rocky cliff-top. It was besieged and damaged during the Civil War.

SHERBORNE, Dorset. An early twelfth-century castle featuring a substantial gatehouse. It was later owned by Sir Walter Ralegh who built a Tudor mansion in the grounds.

STOKESAY, Shropshire. This picturesque fortified manor house was largely built in the thirteenth century by a rich wool merchant.

TAMWORTH, Staffordshire. Of the original Norman motte-and-bailey castle, the large motte survives, on which a seventeenth-century house was built.

TATTERSHALL, Lincolnshire. The surviving remains are largely fifteenth-century, including a massive brick-built tower.

TOTNES, Devon. This large motte-and-bailey castle has a shell-keep on top of the motte.

WARKWORTH *(above)*, Northumberland. The castle is dominated by a massive fourteenth-century tower, built on the site of the motte.

WARWICK, Warwickshire. The castle has been in continuous occupation since the Middle Ages, and has an impressive fourteenth-century facade.

WINDSOR, Berkshire. From its Norman foundation onwards, this has been a very large and important castle. It has a motte and, unusually, two baileys. It was massively redeveloped by Edward III (see pages 56–57) and significant restoration work was carried out in the nineteenth century.

YORK *(above)*, North Yorkshire. Two Norman castles were built on either side of the River Ouse, but only one survived through the Middle Ages as a functioning castle. On top of its motte is a unique quatrefoil tower, known as Clifford's Tower.

Sites in the care of English Heritage. Telephone 0171 973 3434 for details.

INDEX

ACKNOWLEDGEMENTS. **English Heritage would like to thank:**

Brian Davison OBE and Nick Kavanagh for advice; Terry Ball, Tracey Croft, Judith Dobie, Peter Dunn and Ivan Lapper for permission to reproduce their illustrations.

The author has made use of the following books: *A History of the King's Works* vols 1-2, ed H M Colvin (HMSO, 1913); *A Baronial Household in the Thirteenth Century* by M W Labarge (Harvester, 1980); *Henry II* by W L Warren (Eyre Methuen, 1973); *War and Chivalry* by M Strickland (Cambridge University Press, 1996); *The Plantagenet Chronicles* ed E Hallam (Tiger, 1995); *English Historical Documents* vol 2, ed D C Douglas and G W Greenaway (Routledge, 1996); and *English Historical Documents* vol 3, ed H Rothwell (Routledge, 1996).

Picture credits:
Bibliothèque Inguimbertine, Carpenteras 11b; **Bibliothèque Municipale de Chateauroux** 37b; **Bibliothèque Royale Albert 1er, Brussels** 57t; **British Library** 8c (Harley 642 f9v), 9tr, 9br (Add 47682 f6r), 11t (Roy 14E 111 f89), 13t (Add 489/6 fig 50), 14r (Add 42130 f206v), 14b (Add 42130 f63), 15c (Add 42130 f207v), 16b, 18b (Arundel 157 f71v), 20tr, 21r (Add 42130 f159), 22t, 22–23, 23br (Roy 15E 1V f316v), 28t (Cott Nero Ms), 28c, 29c (Roy 10E 1V f202), 30l (Royal 15D 111 f15v), 32t (Cott Nero D1 f182), 35c (Roy 1V f289), 39b (Cott Nero D1 f3), 40–41, 42–43 (Roy 14E 1V f57), 44b

(Ms 48 f168v), 46t, 50b (Roy 20C V11 f133), 54t (Add 42130 f164), 54c (Roy 20C V11 f41v), 55cr (Roy 20E); **British Museum** 17tr, 19r, 35t, 36c, 38t, 39t, 40tl, 44tl, 45tr; **Bridgeman Art Library** 6tl, 9c, 10t, 12t, 13bl, 14t, 15b, 17b, 20t, 20b, 21t, 37br, 38b, 40b, 43b, 45tl, 49c, 56c; **Bodleian Library, Oxford** 12–13 (Bodley 24 f82v), 13br (Bodley 162 B.2.3), 25t (Junius X1 f 81), 41t (Laud misc 653 f5); **Burrell Collection** 37tr; **CADW** 13tl, 27br, 30bl, 31b, 33l, 59cl, 62bl, 62c; **The Master and Fellows, Corpus Christi College, Cambridge** 40tr, 45br, 51b, 52t, 53br, 53bl, 55b; **Chapter & Dean of Canterbury** 33t; **College of Arms** 57cb; **Cumbria Record Office** 29t; **Editions Gaud** 52b; **ET Archive** 46br, 48c, 51t, 61t; **Hampshire County Council** 38t; **Hedingham Castle** 44tr; **John Rylands Library** 33c; **Le Mans Bibliothèque Municipale** 36t, 52c; **Leeds Castle** 6–7; **Michael Holford** 23bl, 24–25, 25r, 28b, 34t; **Medway Council** 42cl; **Museum of London** 53c, 57ct; **National Monuments Record** 8tr; **Christ Church College, Oxford** 42t, 43t; **Pitkin Unichrome** 22b; **Public Record Office** 30rt, 48r; **Royal Collection** 56b; **Royal Armouries** 58t; **Sonia Halliday** 17c, 27c, 32b; **Trustees of Carisbrooke Museum** 10c; **V&A** 6tl, 12b, 18–19, 39c; **Weidenfeld & Nicholson archive** 31t; **Wurttembergisch Landesbibliothek, Stuttgart** 34c; **York City Art Gallery** 58b. All other photographs are the copyright of English Heritage (telephone 0171-973 3338 for details).

Every effort has been made to trace the copyright holders and we apologise in advance for any unintentional omission, which we would be pleased to correct in any subsequent edition of this book.